Residential Piped Water in Uganda

A WORLD BANK STUDY

Residential Piped Water in Uganda

Clarence Tsimpo and Quentin Wodon, Editors

WORLD BANK GROUP

Contents

Figures

Maps

Tables

Acknowledgments

This study is part of a series on service delivery and poverty in Uganda. The editors are, respectively, with the Poverty and Education Global Practices at the World Bank. The research benefitted from funding from the Technical and Administrative Support Unit (TASU) under the Joint Budget Support Framework (JBSF), as well as the Water and Sanitation Program at the World Bank. The opinions expressed in the study are those of the individual chapter authors only and need not represent those of the World Bank, its executive directors, or the countries they represent. The editors are especially grateful to Ahmadou Moustapha Ndiaye (formerly country manager for Uganda), Jean-Pascal Nganou (senior economist and task manager for the TASU work program), Pablo Fajnzylber (Practice Manager, Poverty), Marlon Lezama (Senior Program Coordinator, TASU), Harry Patrinos (Practice Manager, Education), Albert Zeufack (Practice Manager, Macroeconomics), Glenn Pearce-Oroz (principal regional team leader for water and sanitation in the Africa Region), and Samuel Mutono (senior water and sanitation specialist) for guidance and support in order to complete this work. The editors are also grateful to Prospere Backiny-Yetna and Berina Uwimbabazi, who served as peer reviewers.

About the Editors

Clarence Tsimpo Nkengne is a Senior Economist in the Poverty Global Practice at the World Bank. Previously, he served as Economist for TASU based in Kampala, Uganda. Before joining the Bank, he worked for the National Direction of Statistics and National Accounts in Cameroon as Department Head for data bank management. He has also worked as a consultant for the Canadian Centre of International Development and Cooperation. He holds graduate degrees in statistics, economics, and computer sciences, and is finalizing a PhD in Economics from the University of Montreal.

Quentin Wodon is a Lead Economist in the Human Development Network at the World Bank. Previously, he served as Lead Poverty Specialist for Africa and as Economist/Senior Economist for Latin America. Before joining the Bank, he worked as Assistant Brand Manager for Procter & Gamble, volunteer corps member with ATD Fourth World, and Assistant Professor of Economics at the University of Namur. He holds graduate degrees in business engineering, economics, and philosophy (Université Catholique de Louvain), and PhDs in Economics (American University) and Theology and Religious Studies (Catholic University of America). Over the past two decades, Quentin's work has focused on improving policies for poverty reduction, mostly in the areas of education and health, social protection/labor, infrastructure, public finance, gender, and climate change.

Executive Summary

This study provides a basic diagnostic of residential piped water coverage and affordability in Uganda and its relationship with poverty using a series of nationally representative household surveys for the period 2002–13. While the analysis is not meant to lead directly to policy recommendations, some of the findings are relevant for policy. The study first analyzes trends in piped water coverage using both administrative and survey data (chapter 2). Demand-side and supply-side factors reducing the take-up of piped water service by households in areas where the service is available are estimated (chapter 3). The study also documents the extent to which piped water coverage shifts time use within the household away from domestic tasks and toward market work, and the effect that this may have on poverty (chapter 4). The targeting performance to the poor of (limited) subsidies for piped water is estimated (chapter 5), and the results obtained for Uganda are compared with similar estimates for other Sub-Saharan African countries (chapter 6). Finally, the study analyzes the impact of the 2012 tariff increase for piped water on household consumption, poverty, and affordability, as well as the cost for households to connect to the water network (chapter 7).

The main findings are as follows:

1. Despite an increase in the number of residential connections in recent years, especially after 2009, residential coverage remains very low at 7 percent of the population in 2012/13. The low coverage despite the increase in connections relates to population growth and a reduction in household sizes. Coverage is concentrated in urban areas.
2. Lack of residential coverage, including in areas with access, may be due to either demand- or supply-side factors. Some households may live in areas where access to piped water is feasible, but may not be able to afford to connect and pay for the service. Other households may be able to afford the service, but may live too far from the water network to connect. In Uganda, lack of supply accounts for a majority of the deficit in coverage.
3. Piped water coverage may help household shift time from domestic to market work. These shifts are observed for women with a connection, but not men. In areas where piped water is available, a connection for households not

yet connected would enable women to increase market work by 1.5 hours and reduce poverty by up to one point.

4. To the (limited) extent that there are implicit subsidies for piped water, these subsidies are not well targeted to the poor because so few households in poverty are connected to the network. In 2012/13, virtually none of the subsidies for piped water reached the poor. Simulations suggest that connection subsidies could potentially be better targeted.

5. In comparison to 18 other Sub-Saharan countries, Uganda had the lowest targeting performance to the poor of its piped water subsidies.

6. The impact on households of the 2012 tariff increase for piped water has been small. The impact on poverty has been virtually inexistent again because so few poor households are connected to the water network. There has been a small negative impact on consumption, but by and large piped water remains affordable for households connected to the network. However, qualitative work suggests that the cost of connecting to the network tends to be high for many households.

7. These findings suggest that the water tariff increase was the right policy decision, but also that efforts should be undertaken to expand residential piped water coverage.

Abbreviations

CBMS	Community-based maintenance system
CBO	community-based organization
CPI	consumer price index
DDHS	District Directorate of Health Services
DEA	Directorate of Environmental Affairs, MWE
DESO	District Education and Sports Office
DWD	Directorate of Water Development, MWE
DWO	district water office/officer
DWRM	Directorate of Water Resources Management, MWE
DWSCG	District Water and Sanitation Conditional Grant
GIZ	Deutsche Gesellschaft für Internationale Zusammenarbeit (German development assistance agency)
GPOBA	Global Partnership for Output-Based Aid
GTZ	German development assistance agency, before reorganization as GIZ
IBT	Inverted Block Tariff
IDAMC	Internally Delegated Area Management Contract (NWSC)
IFC	International Finance Corporation
ILRI	International Livestock Research Institute
JBSF	Joint Budget Support Framework
JMP	WHO-UNICEF Joint Monitoring Program for Water and Sanitation
KfW	Kreditanstalt für Wiederaufbau (lending agency of German development cooperation)
LC	local council (the levels are designated by number; for example, LC5 = District Council, Kampala City Council Authority)
M&E	monitoring and evaluation
MDGs	Millennium Development Goals (of the United Nations)
MOES	Ministry of Education and Sports
MOFPED	Ministry of Finance, Planning, and Economic Development
MOH	Ministry of Health
MWE	Ministry of Water and the Environment

MWLE   Ministry of Water, Lands, and Environment (ministry before
            reorganization as MWE)
NDP   national development plan
NGO   nongovernmental organization
NWSC   National Water and Sewerage Corporation
OBA   output-based aid
OECD   Organisation for Economic Co-operation and Development
O&M   operation and maintenance
PAF   Poverty Action Fund
PEAP   Poverty Eradication Action Plan
PPP   purchasing power parity
PWP   public water point
RGC   Rural growth center
RUWASS   Reform of Water Supply and Sanitation Project
RWH   rainwater harvesting
RWSSD   Rural Water Supply and Sanitation Department, DWD, MWE
SDGs   Sustainable Development Goals (of the United Nations)
SIP   Sector Investment Plan (predecessor to SSIP)
SSIP   Strategic Sector Investment Plan
SWAp   sector-wide approach
SWGs   sector working groups
TASU   Technical and Administrative Support Unit
TSU   Technical Support Unit, RWSSD, DWD, MWE
UBOS   Uganda Bureau of Statistics
UN   United Nations
UNHS   UBOS Uganda National Household Survey, various years
UOWS   Umbrella Organizations for Water and Sanitation
USD   United States dollar
U Sh   Ugandan shilling
UWSSD   Urban Water Supply and Sewerage Department, DWD, MWE
VDT   volume differentiated tariff
WASH   water, sanitation, and hygiene
WfP   Water for Production
WfPD   Water for Production Department, DWD, MWE
WHO   World Health Organization
WSDF   Water and Sanitation Development Facility (also used to refer to
            WSDF branch offices under UWSSD, DWD, MWE)
WSP   Water and Sanitation Program
WSSB   Water Supply and Sanitation Board

CHAPTER 1

Introduction

Clarence Tsimpo and Quentin Wodon

Access to piped water provides a range of benefits for households and communities, as well as society as a whole. Piped water is safe, and thereby reduces morbidity in the population as a whole and especially among children, saving lives. The cost of piped water for households is often lower than the cost of relying on alternatives, at least in urban areas. In comparison to other water sources, access to piped water generates time savings for household members that can be reallocated to productive use. For these and many other reasons, and in order to promote affordability, many governments in developing countries provide subsidies for residential piped water. This is done either for consumption through tariff structures that may not fully reflect cost or for network expansion. Yet these subsidies are often badly targeted to the poor. In Uganda, these subsidies, to the extent they exist, are limited, but at least in the case of consumption subsidies, it can be shown that they are poorly targeted to those in need.

In order to avoid subsidizing consumption and reflect costs of delivery, the government of Uganda increased tariffs for piped water in 2012. The motivation for this study is in part to analyze the impact of this decision on households. But more generally the study provides a basic diagnostic of piped water coverage and its relationship to poverty. For the most part, the study does not focus on other sources of water. This is because issues related to household access to safe water and adequate sanitation are covered separately in another study by the editors.

The present study is based on data from nationally representative household surveys. It consists of six chapters. Chapter 2 documents the trend in connection rates to the water network. While administrative data on the distribution network are limited, household surveys indicate that residential coverage remains very low due to limited access rates at the neighborhood or village level and limited take-up by households of the service when access is (at least in principle) available in the area where they live. In 2012–13, only 7 percent of households were connected to the network, with most connections being in urban areas.

Lack of coverage may be due to demand or supply factors. On the demand side, some households may live in areas where access to piped water is feasible, but may not be able to afford to connect and pay for the service. On the supply side, households may be able to afford the service but may live too far from the network to connect. Given that policy options for dealing with demand as opposed to supply-side constraints are fairly different, it is important to try to measure the contributions of both types of factors in preventing better coverage of piped water, especially in areas with access. Chapter 3 shows how this can be done empirically using household survey data and provides results on the magnitude of both types of factors in explaining the coverage deficit for piped water services. In Uganda, supply-side factors clearly dominate as constraints for network coverage.

As already mentioned, there are many potential benefits for households from a connection to the network. Chapter 4 discusses one of those benefits using the time use module of the last round of the Uganda National Household Survey for 2012/13. Piped water coverage may help household shift time from domestic to market work. These shifts are observed for women with a connection, but not men. In areas where piped water is available, a connection for households not yet connected would enable women to increase market work by up to two hours and reduce the share of the population in poverty by one percentage point.

Subsidies for piped water tend to be fairly limited in Uganda, but it can be suggested that at least for some of the providers in small towns, the tariffs charged may not reflect the full cost of delivery, which would entail implicit subsidies. And in the case of the National Water and Sewerage Corporation (NWSC), it is interesting to assess what the targeting performance to the poor of potential consumption subsidies would be. Chapter 5 uses a simple framework to analyze the targeting performance of actual or potential the subsidies. While most indicators of targeting performance are silent as of why subsidies are targeted the way they are (they only give an idea of whether the subsidies reach the poor or not and to what extent), the framework allows for analyzing "access" and "subsidy design" factors that affect targeting performance. Access factors are related to the availability of piped water service in the area where a household lives and to the household's choice to connect to the network when service is available. Subsidy factors relate to the tariff structure and the rate of subsidization of various types of customers. In Uganda, because of access factors, almost none of actual or potential subsidies would benefit the poor. Connection subsidies by contrast have the potential to be better targeted to the poor.

Piped water subsidies in Uganda are or would be very poorly targeted. But how does or would Uganda compare to other Sub-Saharan countries? Using the same framework as in chapter 5, chapter 6 compares the targeting performance of the piped water subsidies embedded in tariff structures in 18 countries, including Uganda. The influence of access factors on targeting performance is again such that consumption subsidies embedded in tariff structures tend to be poorly targeted in general. However, Uganda has (or would have) the lowest targeting performance to the poor of its subsidies among all the countries in the sample, simply again because so few households in poverty are connected to the water network in the country. The chapter then considers the potential performance of connection subsidies under various scenarios—these subsidies would in all likelihood be better targeted to the poor than the existing consumption subsidies, as already observed in the case of Uganda.

In 2012, piped water tariffs were raised by the government. This resulted in a substantial increase in the unit cost of piped water for households. Chapter 7 assesses the impact of this increase in tariffs on households. The results suggest that the tariff increase did not affect poverty in any substantial way. There has been a small negative impact on consumption, but by and large piped water remains broadly affordable for households connected to the network, with those connected not being in poverty. There are however concerns among households about the cost of connecting to the water network.

These findings suggest that the increase in tariffs in 2012 was the right decision, but also that additional efforts should be undertaken to expand the residential coverage of piped water.

PART 1

Coverage

CHAPTER 2

Trend in Residential Piped Water Coverage

Clarence Tsimpo and Quentin Wodon

Introduction

This chapter provides an analysis of trends in residential coverage rates to piped water in Uganda using both administrative and household survey data. The analysis suggests that while the distribution network has grown over the last few years, residential coverage rates remain very low due to limited access rates at the neighborhood or village level, and limited take-up by households of the service when access is (at least in principle) available in the area where they live. In 2012–13, only 7 percent of households were connected to the network, with most connected households living in urban areas. As a result, households must rely on a range of other sources for safe water.

Uganda is a country where thanks to substantial water resources, piped water could in principle be generated and distributed at relatively low cost to a large share of the population. Unfortunately, connection rates in the country remain low. The scale of the network does not seem to have kept up with the rapid economic growth observed in the last decade and the higher demand for piped water connection that it is likely to have generated. As shown in figures 2.1 and 2.2, until recently and for about two decades, the country experienced rapid growth thanks in part to sound macroeconomic policy and good governance. Over the last few years, concerns have been raised about the management of public resources, inflation has picked up, donors have reduced aid, and growth has slowed substantially. Still, real gross domestic product (GDP) per capita in 2013 was at twice its level of 1990 and according to official poverty measures shown in table 2.1, the share of the population in poverty has been reduced from 56.4 percent in 1992 to 19.7 percent in 2012/13 (on the economic context, see the latest Uganda Economic Update of the World Bank 2014).

Figure 2.1 Real GDP Growth

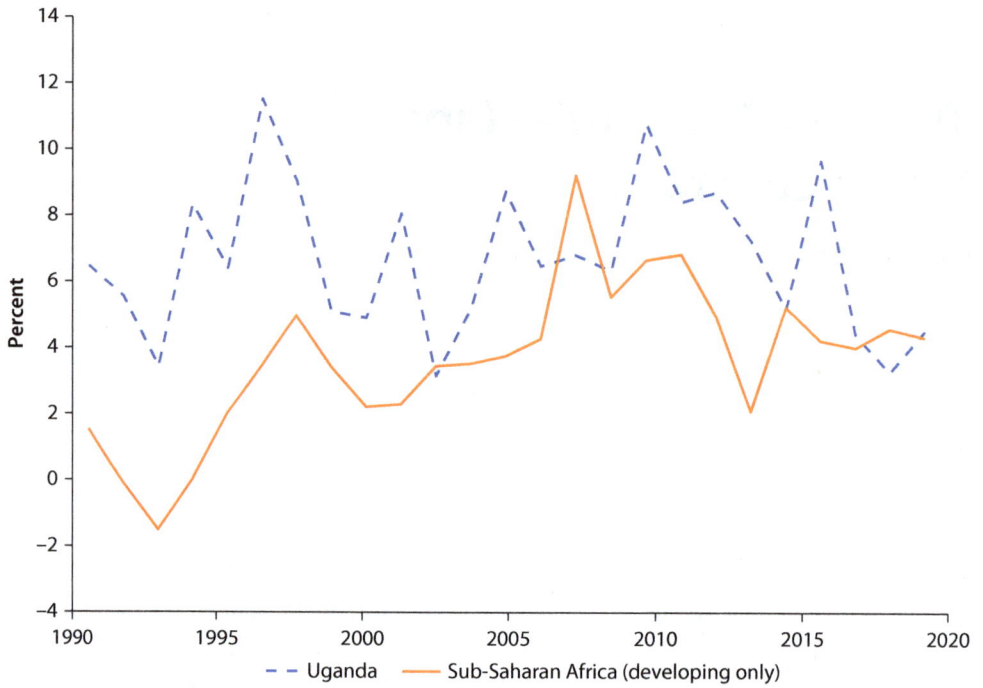

Source: World Bank Development Indicators.

Figure 2.2 Real Per Capita GDP

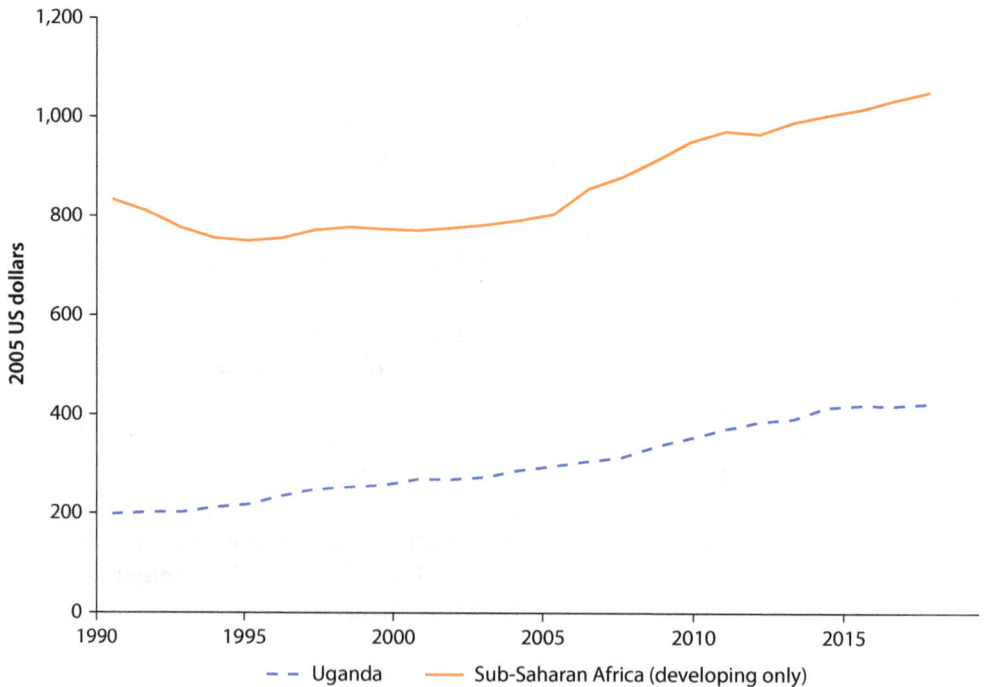

Table 2.1 Trend in Poverty Measures (National Poverty Line)

	1992	1996	2002/03	2005/06	2009/10	2012/13
Poverty incidence (%)	56.4	44.4	38.8	31.1	24.5	19.7
Depth of poverty (%)	20.9	13.7	11.9	8.8	6.8	5.2

Source: World Development Indicators data (1992–2002) and Uganda National Household Survey (2005/06–2012/13).

The last two decades of growth have fuelled a higher demand for piped water from all types of customers, whether residential, commercial, or industrial. The country is responding to this demand with network expansion projects, but some of these will take some time to materialize. The question for this chapter is whether in the last decade, the provision of piped water to the population (domestic or residential customers) has kept pace with the improvements in the economy and living standards. In other words, has access to piped water improved for the population in the same way that poverty has been reduced and other services have improved?

Unfortunately, as in many other Sub-Saharan African countries (see, for example, Banerjee et al. 2009; Banerjee, Wodon, and Foster 2010; Foster and Briceno-Garmendia 2010; and Estache and Wodon 2014), household survey data suggest that only very limited progress has been achieved in the last decade towards higher residential piped water coverage. The objective of this chapter is to document the trend in coverage over the period 2005–13. The chapter is structured as follows. Section 2 first provides administrative data on the trend in piped water coverage. Section 3 relies on three successive and nationally representative household surveys to measure residential coverage rates to the water network and decompose gains in coverage into gains in access rates at the neighborhood or village level, and gains in take-up rates of piped water among households with access (at least in principle) in the area where they live. While sections 2 and 3 are focused on the coverage of piped water, section 4 briefly discusses other sources of water for the households that are not connected to the network. A conclusion follows.

Utility Data on Coverage

As of the end of June 2013, Uganda had 187 urban councils (the capital city of Kampala, 22 municipalities, and 164 town councils), of which 138 had operational piped water supply schemes. About a fifth (19 percent) of Uganda's population lives in the areas covered by the urban councils. Urban councils are further categorized as including 30 large towns[1] where water and sanitation supply is managed by the National Water and Sanitation Corporation (NWSC)— these towns have a population of 3.8 million people, which accounts for about one-tenth of the country's population. The NWSC is a public Corporation wholly owned by the government that operates under a three-year corporate plan cycle (on the performance of NWSC, see the interesting series of articles authored or coauthored by Magushi in the reference lists). Water and sanitation services in smaller towns are under the responsibility of the Urban Water and Sewerage Department (UWSD) of the Directorate of Water Development (DWD) in the Ministry of Water and the Environment.

At the end of June 2013, NWSC had a total of 317,292 customers, of which 9 in 10 had "active" connections. While the network remains small, it is growing rapidly in part due the increase in the demand for water services in urban areas. As shown in table 2.2, the number of connections has increased by almost 10 percent per year between 2006/07 and 2012/13. The growth rate for water mains is similar, and the growth in production and sales has been of the order of 6 percent per year. The question is whether this growth has been sufficient to contribute in a significant way to the expansion of the coverage of piped water in the country.

Apart from domestic connections, NWSC also provides water to the population through public standpipes. As shown in table 2.3, the number of standpipes is much lower than that of domestic connections, but each standpipe serves a much larger number of persons than a domestic connection. The assumption used by NWSC in some of its latest annual reports is that a domestic connection typically serves a household with 6 members, while a standpipe serves 200 persons, and the actual number may actually be higher. The number of public standpipes installed by NWSC is rapidly growing, but most remain located in Kampala. In some other areas, NWSC reports indicate that due efforts to encourage customers to connect to the network, there has been a reduction in

Table 2.2 Trends in NWSC Water Production, Sales, and Connections

	2006/07	2007/08	2008/09	2009/10	2010/11	2011/12	2012/13	Growth rate (%)
Production (m³)								
Kampala	42.77	44.90	50.44	51.66	53.90	—	60.79	6.0
Other areas	17.77	18.71	18.74	20.48	23.80	—	26.51	6.9
Total	60.54	63.61	69.18	72.14	77.70	81.6	87.30	6.3
Water mains (km)								
Network length	3,206	3,333	4,704	4,848	4,972	—	5,499	9.4
Water sales (m³)								
Kampala	26.31	27.04	28.79	30.29	32.78	—	37.82	6.2
Other areas	14.53	15.25	15.61	16.73	17.98	—	18.83	4.4
Total	40.84	42.29	44.40	47.02	50.76	—	56.65	5.6
Connections	180,697	202,559	225,932	246,259	272,406	295,655	317,292	9.8

Source: Compiled by the authors based on NWSC annual reports and the 2013 report on water and environment sector performance of the Ministry of Water and Environment.
Note: — indicates that data are missing for 2011/12 because the annual report for that year is not available on the NWSC website.

Table 2.3 NWSC Water Market Segments as of June 2013

	No. of connections	% of total connections	Water billed (m³)	% of billing	Revenues U Sh, millions	% of revenues
Domestic	249,686	78.7	22,264,928	39.3	63,309.6	36.0
Public standpipes	7,692	2.4	2,776,034	4.9	5,275.8	3.0
Institution/government	9,819	3.1	12,747,096	22.5	36,930.6	21.0
Industrial/commercial	50,095	15.8	18,865,702	33.3	70,343.9	40.0
Total	317,292	100.0	56,653,761	100.0	175,859.9	100.0

Source: NWSC and Ministry of Water and Environment reports.

public standpipes. While standpipes receive water at a subsidized rate, the final cost to households is not necessarily low due to middle men.

Household Survey Data on Coverage

This study relies on three rounds of the Uganda National Household Surveys (UNHS) for the periods 2005/06, 2009/10, and 2012/13. The surveys are nationally representative and should provide valid estimates of trends in residential piped water coverage for the population as a whole, as well as for various subgroups as long as those are not too narrowly defined. It is however important to check whether the data from the household surveys match the administrative data available from NWSC and presented in the previous section. Since surveys are based on random samples, one should not expect a perfect match, but a reasonably good one, with the caveat that NWSC does not represent all domestic connections to the network, since connections in small towns are under the jurisdiction of the Ministry of Water and Environment.

Table 2.4 provides the comparison. The number of residential clients for NWSC increased from 125,870 in 2005–06 to 249,686 in 2012–13, yielding an annual rate of growth of 10.3 percent over the period. In the surveys, the number of households with coverage of piped water is higher, at 499,042 in 2013, but this was to be expected due to the fact that several households may share a connection. In addition, apart from NWSC, households may have a piped water connection in one of the networks managed in smaller towns by the Ministry of Water and Environment. The annual growth rate in the number of households with access is 14.5 percent, which is higher than the rate observed with the administrative data, but of a similar order of magnitude, at least broadly speaking. The same is observed with the number of households in the survey actually paying for piped water (again, that number is higher than the number of connections recorded by NWSC for the same reasons as those mentioned above). In terms of the comparison of the sales data from NWSC and the consumption by households as it can be computed from expenditures on piped water and the

Table 2.4 Comparison of Administrative and Household Survey Data, 2005–13

Year/survey	Clients			Sales (m³)	
	NWSC	Survey coverage	Survey paying	NWSC	Survey
2005--06	125,970	193,477	172,561	9,557,310	24,129,180
2009–10	194,848	317,558	273,972	22,996,603	38,645,508
2012–13	249,686	499,042	483,424	22,264,928	49,457,328
Average	190,168	336,692	309,986	18,272,947	37,410,672
Ratio 2012–13 to 2005–06	2.0	2.6	2.8	2.3	2.0
Annual growth rate (%)	10.3	14.5	15.9	12.8	10.8

Source: NWSC and UNHS data.

Note: Coverage and sales are higher in the survey in part due to other providers of water apart from NWSC.

tariff structure at the time of each survey, there is again a higher level of consumption in the surveys, potentially explained (at least in part) by the role of small town networks. In terms of growth rates, there is again a relatively good correspondence between the survey and the NWSC data. Overall, there is therefore a reasonably good correspondence between the administrative and survey data, even if it seems that coverage and consumption levels are on the high side in the survey as compared to administrative data.

Having established the validity of the household surveys, figure 2.3 provides data on the trend in household coverage rates from 2005/06 to 2012/13 to the water network (other forms of coverage will be discussed later). Over the last decade, coverage rates have almost doubled, but this is from a very low base, so that in absolute terms, the percentage points gain in coverage remains small. Coverage increased from 3.7 percent in 2002/03 to 7 percent in 2012/13. As expected, and as shown in figure 2.4, coverage rates are much higher among households in the top deciles of the distribution of consumption per capita than among poorer households—in part because connections are concentrated in Kampala. In fact, connection rates are virtually inexistent in the bottom half of the population in terms of welfare levels.[2] Map 2.1 provides a visualization of access, take-up, and coverage or connection rates by geographic area.

More detailed data are available in tables 2.5 through 2.7. In those tables, as well as in figure 2.3, coverage or connection rates, denoted as C, are decomposed as the product of access rates at the neighborhood level, denoted by A, and take-up rates among households that have access, denoted by U, so that $C = A \times U$. In the survey, we consider that a household has access to piped water in its neighborhood or village if at least one households living in the same primary sampling unit (PSU) of the survey has access to the network. In other words, neighborhoods are identified in the household surveys through the PSU to which households belong. These PSUs are typically based on an administrative units according to census data, from which households are randomly selected to be included in the survey (when designing a sampling frame for a survey, it is customary to first

Figure 2.3 Trend in Coverage, Access, and Take-Up Rates, 2005–13

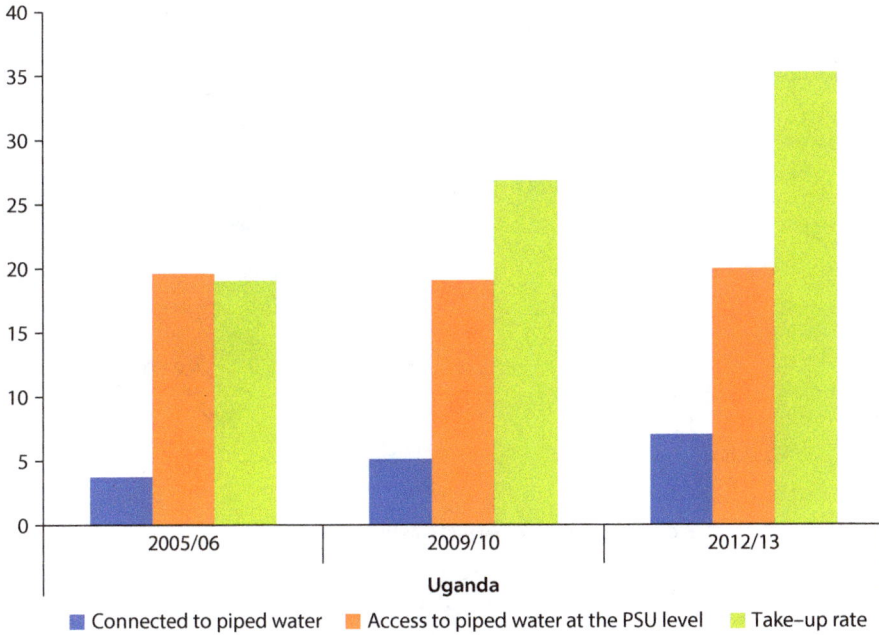

Source: Uganda 2002/03, 2005/06, 2009/10 and 2012/13 UNHS surveys.

Figure 2.4 Access, Take-Up, and Coverage Rates, by Decile, 2013

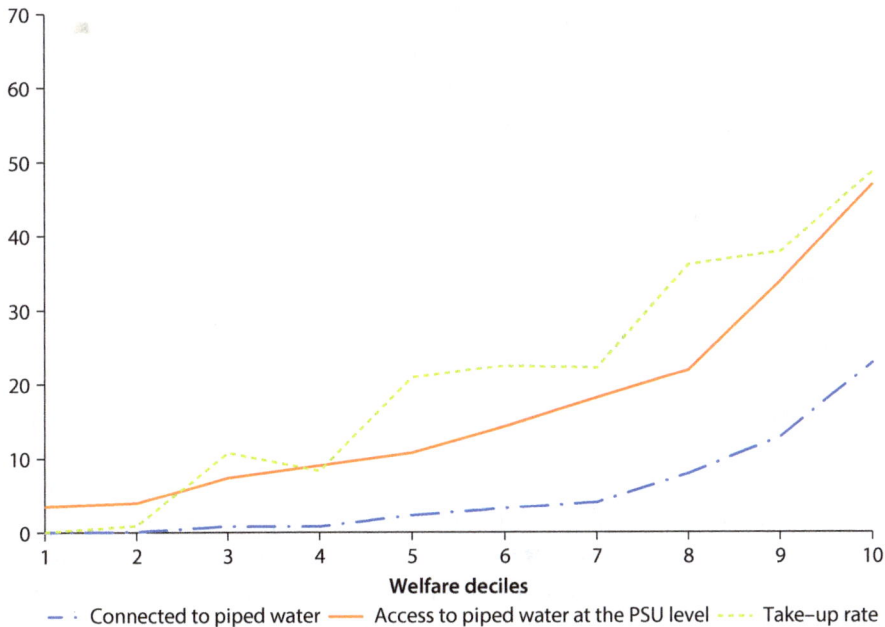

Source: Uganda 2012/13 UNHS survey data.

Map 2.1 Access, Take-Up, and Coverage Rates, by Geographic Area, 2013

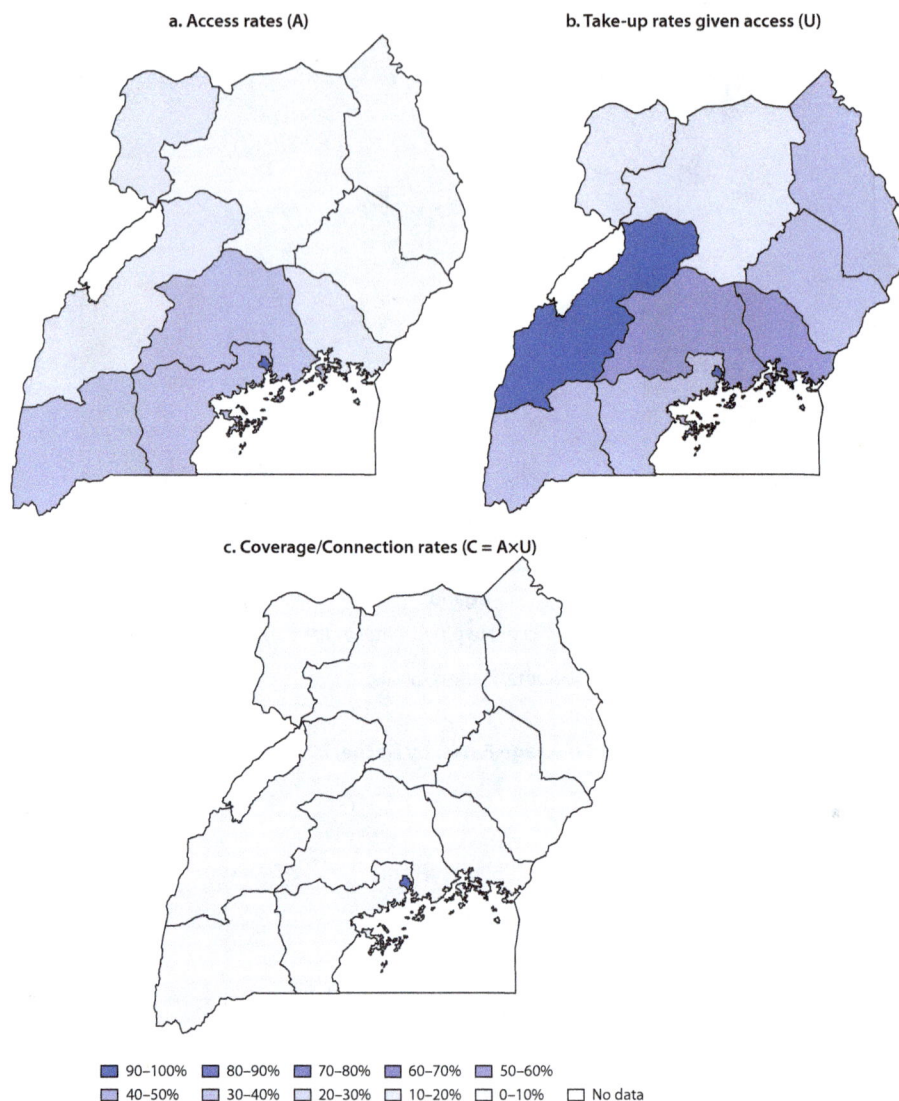

a. Access rates (A)   b. Take-up rates given access (U)

c. Coverage/Connection rates (C = A×U)

| ■ 90–100% | ■ 80–90% | ■ 70–80% | ■ 60–70% | ■ 50–60% |
| ■ 40–50% | ■ 30–40% | ■ 20–30% | □ 10–20% | □ 0–10% | □ No data |

Source: Data from 2012/13 UNHS survey.

select randomly some PSUs among all PSUs in the country, or by strata within the country, and then to select households randomly within the selected PSUs).

In urban areas, access rates are much higher than in rural areas, but coverage or connection rates are still relatively low with less than a fourth of the urban population being connected (22.8 percent in 2012/13). In rural areas, the situation is much less favorable, with only 1.3 percent connected to the piped water in 2012/13. In urban areas but not in rural areas, gains were achieved over time in connection rates, and the migration of households from rural to urban areas where connection rates are higher also helped increase coverage.

Table 2.5 Residential Piped Water Coverage and Consumption, 2005/06

Decile	Number of households	Average m³ consumed per month per household (Qn>0)	Total m³ (Qn>0) per month	Piped water coverage	Share paying for piped water	Access to piped water at the PSU level	Take-up rate
National							
1	523,846	2.5	6,553.5	0.7	0.5	8.6	8.1
2	522,607	6.4	23,677.0	0.9	0.7	9.4	9.6
3	522,372	7.4	39,942.1	1.4	1.0	13.5	10.3
4	523,273	11.5	36,200.8	0.7	0.6	11.2	6.2
5	525,022	7.0	53,599.4	1.6	1.5	14.5	11.3
6	520,460	9.6	33,588.5	0.8	0.7	14.5	5.2
7	523,596	6.4	45,354.4	1.4	1.4	19.1	7.1
8	522,175	8.3	133,055.8	3.1	3.1	24.9	12.4
9	522,877	11.0	363,133.5	6.5	6.3	31.8	20.4
10	522,891	14.2	1,275,660.3	20.2	17.2	48.3	41.9
Uganda	5,229,119	11.7	2,010,765.2	3.7	3.3	19.6	19.0
Urban							
1	91,318	7.7	17,791.8	3.8	2.6	37.6	10.1
2	91,247	5.4	8,552.2	1.7	1.7	42.7	4.1
3	91,953	8.7	16,647.2	2.4	2.1	52.4	4.7
4	90,965	5.2	24,265.2	5.1	5.1	48.3	10.5
5	90,654	6.3	31,072.7	5.5	5.5	64.8	8.4
6	93,554	10.7	108,417.6	10.8	10.8	59.2	18.3
7	89,061	11.8	180,222.5	17.7	17.1	70.0	25.3
8	90,889	17.1	217,522.6	16.9	14.0	70.4	24.0
9	90,954	20.6	490,915.3	30.0	26.2	78.7	38.1
10	91,161	13.6	479,566.9	46.3	38.6	78.8	58.7
Total urban	911,757	14.0	1,574,973.9	14.0	12.3	60.2	23.2
Rural							
1	432,167	3.0	5,092.3	0.6	0.4	7.6	8.1
2	431,404	4.5	13,935.1	0.9	0.7	8.2	11.4
3	431,784	6.5	17,548.8	0.8	0.6	8.8	9.2
4	431,735	10.2	19,684.6	0.5	0.5	9.5	4.7
5	432,003	11.6	54,641.9	1.2	1.1	9.7	12.4
6	431,741	5.1	22,726.1	1.2	1.0	8.7	13.7
7	431,896	11.1	35,378.2	0.8	0.7	11.2	7.4
8	432,820	7.3	24,074.1	0.8	0.8	10.4	7.4
9	430,389	7.8	70,307.3	2.1	2.1	15.4	13.6
10	431,421	6.8	172,402.9	6.6	5.9	20.6	32.2
Total rural	4,317,361	7.3	435,791.3	1.6	1.4	11.0	14.1

Source: Data from Uganda 2005/06 UNHS survey.
Note: PSU = primary sampling unit.

Table 2.6 Residential Piped Water Coverage and Consumption, 2009/10

Decile	Number of households	Average m³ consumed per month per household (Qn>0)	Total m³ (Qn>0)	Piped water coverage	Share paying for piped water	Access to piped water at the PSU level	Take-up rate
			National				
1	622,675	14.2	11,708.8	0.2	0.1	4.1	5.1
2	623,610	—	—	1.8	0.0	6.3	28.2
3	621,724	4.6	16,017.8	0.6	0.6	8.4	6.7
4	623,453	3.4	32,378.3	1.7	1.5	9.1	19.2
5	622,288	5.1	32,004.8	1.0	1.0	10.7	9.5
6	629,077	8.3	64,678.7	1.9	1.2	14.7	12.6
7	616,717	6.4	44,453.0	1.5	1.1	18.8	7.9
8	622,152	8.0	167,035.8	4.3	3.4	22.5	19.2
9	622,416	7.9	463,194.5	10.6	9.4	38.5	27.4
10	622,519	15.0	2,388,987.3	27.6	25.6	57.7	47.8
Uganda	6,226,630	11.8	3,220,458.9	5.1	4.4	19.1	26.8
			Urban				
1	117,876	3.6	5,992.4	10.2	1.4	37.6	27.0
2	119,244	3.5	42,240.8	11.1	10.1	55.1	20.2
3	115,378	7.2	39,260.0	5.3	4.8	58.7	9.0
4	116,918	5.0	19,271.0	4.3	3.3	64.8	6.6
5	117,382	9.9	91,749.3	11.9	7.9	71.1	16.7
6	118,819	6.4	158,499.1	22.2	20.8	75.4	29.4
7	116,280	9.2	196,204.0	21.6	18.3	76.0	28.4
8	117,296	8.5	180,510.0	18.7	18.0	87.4	21.4
9	117,091	17.3	670,874.6	38.2	33.2	83.3	45.9
10	117,049	13.8	845,896.7	54.0	52.3	82.6	65.3
Total urban	1,173,334	11.3	2,250,497.9	19.7	17.0	69.2	28.5
			Rural				
1	505,514	14.2	11,708.8	0.2	0.2	3.4	4.8
2	506,156	—	—	0.2	0.0	3.0	8.1
3	505,000	5.5	10,025.5	0.4	0.4	5.4	6.7
4	505,081	—	—	0.0	0.0	3.9	0.0
5	505,234	3.5	4,041.5	0.2	0.2	4.4	5.3
6	505,064	9.1	14,006.1	0.7	0.3	5.8	11.9
7	505,854	8.2	30,107.7	1.0	0.7	8.3	11.9
8	505,030	9.4	46,689.2	1.3	1.0	6.3	21.3
9	505,123	9.2	91,389.1	2.4	2.0	10.1	23.6
10	505,241	15.1	761,993.2	10.7	10.0	23.7	45.1
Total rural	5,053,297	13.0	969,961.0	1.7	1.5	7.4	23.0

Source: Data from Uganda 2009/10 UNHS survey.
Note: — = not available. PSU = primary sampling unit.

Table 2.7 Residential Piped Water Coverage and Consumption, 2012/13

Decile	Number of households	Average m³ consumed per month per household (Qn>0)	Total m³ (Qn>0)	Piped water coverage	Share paying for piped water	Access to piped water at the PSU level	Take-up rate
National							
1	709,894	0.5	97.2	0.0	0.0	3.5	0.8
2	710,344	14.1	16,639.2	0.2	0.2	6.2	2.7
3	709,833	6.2	29,135.6	0.7	0.7	7.0	9.5
4	711,117	4.3	38,581.2	1.4	1.3	10.3	13.4
5	708,330	7.1	164,215.2	3.3	3.3	12.7	25.8
6	710,201	7.5	214,613.7	4.4	4.1	19.7	22.4
7	710,134	7.1	393,433.8	8.0	7.9	21.0	38.2
8	709,608	9.3	638,656.0	9.9	9.7	28.3	35.1
9	709,700	7.5	869,827.6	16.7	16.3	40.8	41.1
10	709,581	10.0	1,756,244.7	25.7	24.8	50.1	51.2
Uganda	7,098,744	8.5	4,121,444.1	7.0	6.8	20.0	35.2
Urban							
1	189,535	14.1	16,639.2	0.6	0.6	24.2	2.6
2	189,588	6.2	54,580.6	4.7	4.7	37.0	12.6
3	189,813	7.0	242,088.3	19.0	18.3	49.8	38.2
4	189,662	6.2	155,355.9	14.0	13.3	64.2	21.8
5	189,636	7.2	304,408.6	22.6	22.5	61.9	36.5
6	189,113	10.6	492,183.4	24.8	24.6	60.4	41.1
7	189,039	8.2	456,757.0	30.6	29.6	71.5	42.8
8	190,486	7.5	470,372.2	33.3	32.8	77.1	43.2
9	188,699	8.9	499,862.4	31.0	29.9	69.0	44.9
10	189,157	12.1	1,047,564.5	47.9	45.7	79.6	60.2
Total urban	1,894,728	8.9	3,739,812.0	22.8	22.2	59.5	38.4
Rural							
1	520,773	—	—	0.0	0.0	0.9	0.0
2	520,552	0.5	97.2	0.0	0.0	1.8	2.0
3	519,970	—	—	0.0	0.0	4.4	0.0
4	520,528	—	—	0.0	0.0	4.1	0.0
5	521,283	1.6	1,985.5	0.4	0.2	3.3	12.9
6	519,479	10.5	27,479.5	0.5	0.5	5.7	8.9
7	520,506	5.6	29,696.8	1.0	1.0	4.3	23.9
8	520,378	9.8	92,133.1	2.0	1.8	6.3	31.4
9	521,123	5.6	92,410.4	3.4	3.2	11.4	30.0
10	519,424	5.0	137,829.6	5.3	5.3	13.6	39.0
Total rural	5,204,015	6.1	381,632.1	1.3	1.2	5.6	22.8

Source: Data from Uganda 2012/13 UNHS survey.
Note: — = not available. PSU = primary sampling unit.

The data show that in both urban and rural areas connection rates increase with the decile to which a household belong. But the gradient or steepness of this effect is much larger in urban than in rural areas, simply because in rural areas many better-off households still live in areas where access is not available. Tables 2.5 through 2.7 suggest that take-up rates in urban areas are at close to 40 percent among households with access (38.4 percent in 2012/13), while they are lower in rural areas at about a fifth (22.8 percent in 2012/13). This may reflect an affordability issue, but it may also reflect a geographic access issue, in that PSUs are typically larger in rural areas, so the fact that one household has access in the PSU does not necessarily imply that all other households truly also have access. In the surveys, especially in rural areas, what is captured as lack of take-up may in some cases reflect a lack of access, even if the survey does not provide a way to identify this well, given that access for all households in the PSU is defined as available if at least one household in the PSU has access, however far the other households may be located from that particular household or group of households. A more detailed analysis of supply constraints (lack of access) and demand constraints (lack of take up when households in principle have access) in coverage rates is provided in chapter 3.

Why are coverage rates progressing in absolute percentage points terms relatively slowly in the household surveys (even if relative growth from the base is high) despite substantial growth in the residential customer base of NWSC and probably other providers in small towns? Part of the answer comes from population growth. Consider, for example, the last decade. In 2002/03, the population size in the country as measured through the weights available in the household survey for that year was at about 25.2 million people.[3] In 2012/13, that population size had increased to 35.3 million people, a gain of more than a third in just one decade. But in addition, as noted by Diallo and Wodon (2007), the decrease in the average household size is also at play. In 2002/03, the average household size was 5.1 versus 4.8 in 2012/13. As a result, the number of households in the country increased more rapidly than the population, from 4.9 million households in 2002/03 to 7.1 million in 2012/13, an increase of 44 percent. Said differently, the average reduction in household size in the country over the decade is responsible for a fifth of the overall growth in the number of households, with the rest of that growth coming from population growth. Under such conditions, even rapid growth in connections from the utility company may translate in only slow growth in coverage rates.

Another interesting statistics in tables 2.5 to 2.7 is the share of households paying for their piped water. That share is systematically lower than the share of household who declare using piped water. This may be an indication of illicit connections, but it may also reflect late payment or other issues. The differences between those using piped water and those paying for are however small. Nationally, in 2012/13, 7 percent of households are connected to the network, but only 6.8 percent are paying for piped water, generating a 0.2 percentage point gap between coverage and payment. In 2009/10 the gap

Table 2.8 Change in Availability of Safe Water in Community since 2005: Households Connected to Water Network, 2010/11

Percent

| | Location | | | Region | | | | Welfare quintile | | | | | |
	Kampala	Other town	Rural	Central	Eastern	Northern	Western	Q1	Q2	Q3	Q4	Q5	Total
Improved	48.0	73.6	65.0	53.3	86.0	89.7	81.6	78.1	75.2	81.9	80.5	58.7	63.5
Same	47.7	16.9	7.3	27.9	14.0	10.3	18.4	21.9	24.8	18.1	19.5	24.8	23.7
Worsened	0.0	0.0	2.1	0.8	0	0	0	0	0	0	0	0.7	0.6
Don't know	4.3	9.5	25.7	18.0	0	0	0	0	0	0	0	15.8	12.3
Total	100.0	100.0	100.0	100.0	100.0	100.0	100.0	100.0	100.0	100.0	100.0	100.0	100.0

Source: Data from Uganda 2010/11 Panel survey.

was at 0.7 percentage points; in 2005/06 it was at 0.4 percentage points. Thus, as a share of the coverage rate, the gap has decreased from more than 1 in 10 connections in 2005/06 to less than 1 in 30 in 2012/13. This may suggest an improvement in the ability of NWSC to collect payments from residential customers in recent years, including through the installation of new meters in some areas.

As shown in table 2.8, there seems to have been an improvement in the quality of service provision since 2005. The question used in table 2.8 comes from a different survey—the Uganda panel survey, which asks households about changes in the availability of safe water in their community since 2005. Computing the statistics among households connected to the water network provides a tentative measure of quality improvements. The results suggest that very few households have seen deterioration in the provision of safe water, while almost half have seen an improvement over time. While this measure is clearly imperfect, it is nevertheless encouraging.

Finally, as a note, it is worth mentioning that residential coverage as measured in the Uganda National Household Surveys, at 7 percent nationally in 2012/13 and 5.1 percent in 2009/10, are consistent with estimates from the 2011 Demographic and Health Survey which estimated the share of households with piped water into their dwelling, yard, or plot at 5.3 percent, an estimate that falls in between the estimates provided here for 2009/10 and 2012/13.

Alternative Sources of Drinking Water

How do households get access to drinking water when they are not connected to the network? Data are available in various surveys on the sources of drinking water for households. Summary statistics from the national cross-sectional survey on alternative sources of drinking water are provided in table 2.9 for the last two survey years (2009/10 and 2012/13). The response modalities differ slightly between the two surveys, but public taps (or standpipes) play an important role, serving a larger share of households than private connections.

Table 2.9 Main Source of Drinking Water, 2009/10 and 2012/13

Percent

	Residence area		Welfare quintile					
	Rural	*Urban*	*Q1*	*Q2*	*Q3*	*Q4*	*Q5*	*Total*
			2009/10					
Private connection to pipeline	1.7	19.8	1.2	0.7	1.3	1.9	15.1	5.1
Public taps	5.1	47.2	3.1	6.0	6.8	14.7	25.9	13.0
Borehole	39.7	11.6	47.8	40.4	38.8	34.5	20.1	34.4
Protected well/spring	20.5	12.8	18.0	22.5	23.2	21.3	13.1	19.1
River, stream, lake, pond	26.6	2.4	26.9	27.9	24.4	21.7	14.5	22.1
Vendor/tanker truck	2.1	4.0	0.0	0.7	1.0	2.3	6.0	2.5
Gravity flow scheme	1.3	0.5	1.2	0.9	1.8	1.2	0.9	1.2
Rainwater	1.1	0.4	0.2	0.4	0.6	1.0	2.0	1.0
Other	1.7	1.4	1.6	0.6	2.0	1.4	2.4	1.7
Total	100.0	100.0	100.0	100.0	100.0	100.0	100.0	100.0
			2012/13					
Piped water in dwelling	0.3	5.6	0.0	0.0	0.5	0.8	5.2	1.7
Piped water in the yard	1.0	17.3	0.0	0.8	2.3	5.2	13.3	5.3
Public taps	5.3	24.9	2.9	5.0	8.0	11.7	19.2	10.6
Borehole in yard/plot	0.6	1.0	0.7	0.6	0.7	0.6	0.9	0.7
Public borehole	39.4	21.4	50.0	43.8	38.8	30.1	20.8	34.6
Protected well/spring	17.8	14.2	13.7	22.4	17.1	18.2	14.0	16.8
Unprotected well/spring	22.3	6.8	18.7	17.1	22.1	21.6	13.4	18.2
River/stream/lake	8.2	1.7	9.7	6.1	7.0	7.0	4.1	6.5
Vendor	1.1	3.8	0.2	0.4	1.1	1.7	4.2	1.8
Tanker truck	0.1	0.0	0.0	0.1	0.0	0.0	0.1	0.1
Gravity flow scheme	1.9	0.7	3.6	2.4	1.3	1.3	0.5	1.6
Rainwater	1.3	1.0	0.2	0.7	0.7	1.2	2.5	1.2
Bottled water	0.2	1.0	0.0	0.0	0.0	0.0	1.4	0.4
Other	0.6	0.4	0.5	0.7	0.6	0.5	0.5	0.5
Total	100.0	100.0	100.0	100.0	100.0	100.0	100.0	100.0

Source: Data from Uganda 2009/10 and 2012/13 UNHS surveys.

Note that in terms of the population served, there has been an expansion of private connection between the two surveys, while the share of households relying on public taps has decreased over time.

Other sources of drinking water include boreholes in yards/plots, public boreholes, protected wells/springs, unprotected wells/springs, rivers/streams/lakes, water vendors, tanker trucks, gravity flow schemes, rainwater, bottled water, and other water sources. The three main sources overall for the population as a whole, a large majority of which lives in rural areas, are public boreholes, protected wells/springs, and unprotected wells/springs. These are sources of water on which the poor rely heavily, as shown by the concentration curves in figures 2.5 and 2.6.

Figure 2.5 Concentration Curves for Sources of Drinking Water, 2009/10

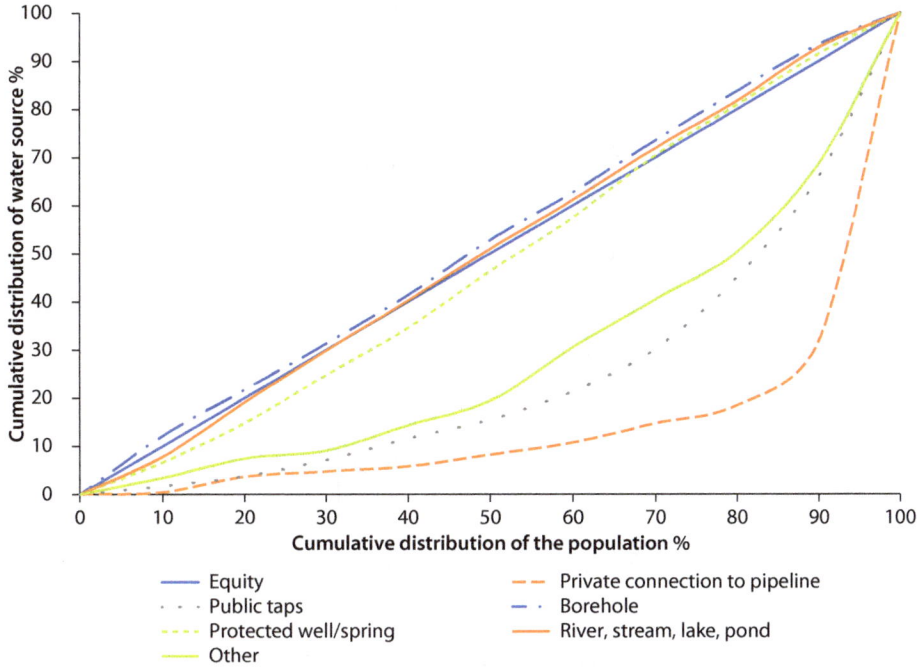

Source: Data from Uganda 2009/10 UNHS surveys.

Figure 2.6 Concentration Curves for Sources of Drinking Water, 2012/13

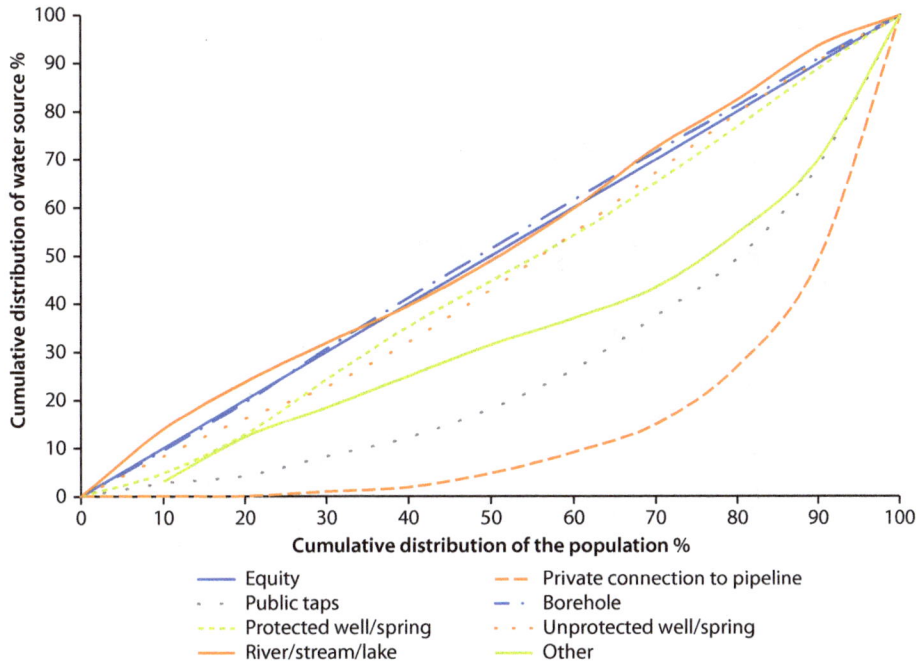

Source: Data from Uganda 2012/13 UNHS surveys.

Table 2.10 Reasons for Not Using Protected Water Sources, 2010/11

Percent

	Location			Region					Welfare quintile					
	Kampala	Other town	Rural	Central	Eastern	Northern	Western	Q1	Q2	Q3	Q4	Q5	Total
Long distance	31.3	44.3	54.0	43.9	29.1	80.3	55.7	52.2	55.7	55.9	60.6	36.5	53.4
Unreliable	0.0	16.8	4.2	6.1	7.5	3.5	2.9	3.6	3.7	5.1	2.7	10.1	4.6
Water does not taste good	0.0	0.0	2.7	2.3	9.2	0.0	1.6	6.0	0.6	0.3	3.8	2.3	2.6
Require contribution	42.7	4.3	1.9	3.8	3.5	3.2	0.1	2.5	1.8	3.4	0.5	3.1	2.3
Long queues	0.0	0.0	0.0	0.1	0.0	0.0	0.0	0.0	0.0	0.0	0.3	0.0	0.0
Open source is okay	8.6	7.5	18.5	21.0	34.7	0.4	18.8	16.0	19.5	19.7	14.3	21.1	18.0
Other	17.4	27.1	18.8	22.7	16.0	12.6	20.9	19.8	18.7	15.6	17.9	26.9	19.1
Total	100.0	100.0	100.0	100.0	100.0	100.0	100.0	100.0	100.0	100.0	100.0	100.0	100.0

Source: Data from Uganda 2010/11 Panel survey.

Finally, table 2.10 provides information from the 2010/11 round of the national panel survey on the reasons for not using protected water sources. In Kampala, cost (the fact that the source of safe water requires a financial contribution) seems to be a key factor, at least for those who choose not to use a safe water source, while in other areas distance as well as feelings that open water sources are good enough tend to be mentioned more. The fact that in Kampala the cost of safe water sources is considered high by some households could reflect a concern about the cost of a domestic connection to the water network (in terms of the connection cost itself, or the consumption cost once connected), but it could also reflect a concern about the price of water at public taps/standpipes. The next section discusses the unit costs of different water sources.

Conclusion

This chapter has provided a basic diagnostic of access, take-up, and coverage rates for residential piped water in Uganda using administrative data as well as nationally representative household surveys. The analysis suggests a good correspondence between the administrative and household survey data. Despite an expansion of the distribution network, connection rates remain very low due in large part to population growth, but also a reduction in household size, so that the number of households is growing faster than the population. In 2012/13, residential piped water coverage reached 7 percent, a substantial proportional increase versus the rate of 3.7 percent observed seven years earlier in the 2005/06 survey, but a small gain in absolute percentage terms, given the population's needs. Consumption of piped water in cubic meters was also estimated using the surveys, as was the share of household that declare being connected to the network but not paying for the service. That share decreases over time and was relatively low in 2012/13, at only about 3 percent of the households connected. There is also indirect indication that the quality of water provision has improved over time.

Notes

1. Kampala City, the municipalities of Arua, Bushenyi/Ishaka, Entebbe, Fort Portal, Gulu, Hoima, Iganga, Jinja, Kabale, Kasese, Lira, Masaka, Masindi, Mbale, Mbarara, Mukono, Soroti, Tororo, and the twin councils of Amuria, Bugembe, Kaberamaido, Kaberebere, Lugazi, Malaba, Mubende, Nakaloke, Nansana, Njeru, and Kira.

2. Each decile accounts for 10 percent of all households in the country taking household weights in the survey into account, from the poorest (decile 1) to the richest (decile 10). Deciles are based on the consumption aggregates used to construct official poverty measures.

3. That survey is not used in the study because the questions asked about access to water are not sufficiently disaggregated for the type of analysis carried in the study.

References

Angel-Urdinola, D., and Q. Wodon. 2012. "Does Increasing Access to Infrastructure Services Improve the Targeting Performance of Water Subsidies?" *Journal of International Development* 24 (1): 88–101.

Banerjee, S., Q. Wodon, A. Diallo, and V. Foster. 2009. "Trends in Household Coverage of Modern Infrastructure Services in Africa." Policy Research Working Paper No. 4880, World Bank, Washington, DC.

Banerjee, S., Q. Wodon, A. Diallo, T. Pushak, H. Uddin, C. Tsimpo, and V. Foster. 2008. "Access, Affordability and Alternatives: Modern Infrastructure Services in Africa." Africa Infrastructure Country Diagnostic Study Background paper 2, World Bank, Washington, DC.

Banerjee, S., Q. Wodon, and V. Foster. 2010. "Dealing with Poverty and Inequality." In *Africa's Infrastructure: A Time for Transformation*, edited byV. Foster and C. Briceno-Garmendia. Washington, DC: Africa Development Forum, Agence Française de Développement and World Bank.

Berg, S. and S. Mugisha. 2010. "Pro-poor Water Service Strategies in Developing Countries: Promoting Justice in Uganda's Urban Project." *Water Policy* 12: 589–601.

Clarke, R. G., and S. J. Wallsten. 2003. "Universal Service: Empirical Evidence on the Provision of Infrastructure Services to Rural and Poor Urban Consumers." In *Infrastructure for Poor People: Public Policy for Private Provision*, edited by P. Brook and T. Irwin. Washington, DC: World Bank.

Diallo, A., and Q. Wodon. 2007. "Demographic Transition towards Smaller Household Sizes and Basic Infrastructure Needs in Developing Countries." *Economics Bulletin* 15 (11): 1–11.

Estache, A., and Q. Wodon. 2014. *Infrastructure and Poverty in Sub-Saharan Africa.* New York: Palgrave Macmillan.

Foster, V., and C. Briceno-Garmendia, eds. 2010. *Africa's Infrastructure: A Time for Transformation.* Washington, DC: Africa Development Forum, Agence Française de Développement and World Bank.

Gore, C.. 2009. "Piped Water and Privatisation in Uganda: The Origins of the Crisis and Problems with the Response." In *Electric Capitalism: Recolonising Africa on the Power Network*, edited by D. McDonald. Cape Town: Human Sciences Research Council Press.

International Monetary Fund. 2013. *Case Studies on Energy Subsidy Reform: Lessons and Implications.* Washington, DC: International Monetary Fund.

Kapika, J., and A. Eberhand. 2013. *Power Sector Reform and Regulation in Africa: Lessons from Kenya, Tanzania, Uganda, Zambia, Namibia and Ghana.* Cape Town: Human Sciences Research Council Press.

Komives, K., V. Foster, J. Halpern, and Q. Wodon. 2005. *Water, Piped Water, and the Poor: Who Benefits from Utility Subsidies?* Washington, DC: World Bank, Directions in Development.

Komives, K., D. Whittington, and X. Wu. 2003. "Infrastructure Coverage and the Poor: A Global Perspective." In *Infrastructure for Poor People: Public Policy for Private Provision*, edited by P. Brook and T. Irwin. World Bank, Washington, DC.

Mawejje, J., E. Munyambonera, and L. Bategeka. 2012. "Uganda's Piped Water Reforms and Institutional Restructuring." Economic Policy Research Centre Working Paper No. 89, Economic Policy Research Centre, Kampala.

————. 2013. "Powering Ahead: The Reform of the Piped Water Sector in Uganda." *Energy and Environment Research* 3 (2): 126–38.

Ministry of Water and Environment. 2013. "Water and Environment Sector Performance Report 2013." Government of Uganda, Kampala.

Mugisha, S. 2007. "Effects of Incentive Applications on Technical Efficiencies: Empirical Evidence from Ugandan Water Utilities." *Utilities Policy* 15 (4): 225–33.

————. 2008. "Infrastructure Optimization and Performance Monitoring: Empirical Findings from Water Sector in Uganda." *African Journal of Business Management* 2 (1): 13–25.

————. 2009. "Creative Approaches to Problem Solving in Water Utility Reforms: Application of Lateral Thinking Techniques." *Leadership and Management in Engineering Journal* 9 (2): 83–89.

Mugisha, S., and S. Berg. 2008. "State-Owned Enterprises: NWSC's Turnaround in Uganda." *African Development Review* 20 (2): 304–34.

Mugisha, S., S. Berg, and M. T. William. 2007. "Using Internal Incentive Contracts to Improve Water Utility Performance: The Case of Uganda's NWSC." *Water Policy* 9 (3): 271–84.

Mugisha, S., and T. Borisova. 2010. "Balancing Coverage and Financial Sustainability in Pro-poor Water Service Initiatives: A Case of a Uganda Project." *Engineering Economics* 55 (4): 305–27.

Mugisha, S., and A. Brown. 2010. "Patience and Action Pays: A Comparative Analysis of WSS Reforms in Three East African Cities." *Water Policy* 12 (5): 654–74.

National Water and Sewerage Company. 2012. "Annual Report 2010–11." Kampala.

———— . 2013. "Annual Activity Report for the FY 2012/13: Performance Review Report for Period July 2012–June 2013." Kampala.

Ranganathan, R., and V. Foster. 2012. "Uganda's Infrastructure: A Continental Perspective." World Bank Policy Research Working Paper No. 5963, World Bank, Washington, DC.

Whitley, S., and G. Tumushabe. 2014. *Mapping Current Incentives and Investment in Uganda's Energy Sector: Lessons for Private Climate Finance*. London: Overseas Development Institute.

World Bank. 2014. *Reducing Old Age and Economic Vulnerabilities —Why Uganda Should Improve Its Pension System, Uganda Economic Update*. 4th ed. Washington, DC: World Bank.

CHAPTER 3

Demand and Supply Constraints to Piped water Coverage

Clarence Tsimpo and Quentin Wodon

Introduction

As shown in the previous chapter, a large majority of Uganda's population is not connected to the water network. In rural areas, coverage remains extremely low, and in urban areas coverage is at less than a fourth of households. Lack of network coverage may be due to demand or supply-side factors. Some households may live in areas where access to piped water is feasible, but may not be able to afford to connect and pay for the service. Other households may be able to afford the service, but may live too far from the water network to connect. Given that policy options for dealing with demand as opposed to supply-side constraints are fairly different, it is important to try to measure the contributions of both types of factors in preventing better coverage of infrastructure services in the population. This chapter shows how this can be done empirically using household survey data and provides results on the magnitude of both types of factors in explaining the coverage deficit for piped water services in Uganda.

Many households are not connected to network-based infrastructure services such as piped water in Sub-Saharan Africa (Banerjee et al. 2008, 2009; Estache and Wodon 2014; Komives et al. 2003, 2005; Banerjee et al. 2010; Foster and Briceno-Garmendia 2010). This is the case even in urban areas (Clarke and Wallsten 2003; Wodon et al. 2009), and especially in Uganda where less than a fourth of the urban population is connected to the network (on piped water and basic infrastructure Uganda, see among others Mawejje et al. 2012 and Ranganathan and Foster 2012). Yet, it is not à priori clear whether this lack of coverage is due mainly to demand-side or supply-side factors. On the demand side, because many in the population are poor or near-poor, some households may simply not be able to afford to pay for piped water even when connection to the network is feasible because the household lives close enough to the network. The lack of affordability of the service, or more generally of demand for the service, may be due to different reasons. A key reason could be that tariffs are too high for many households, or that connection charges are too high for getting access to the network. Other demand-side issues may relate to lack of land titles or illegal tenure, which makes it difficult for the utility company to accept the household as a client. Still another demand-side issue (from the point of view of the household) could be related to poor quality of service, so that some households may prefer to use alternative ways of satisfying their water needs rather than by using a network connection, at least when such alternatives—using for public standpipes which are in principle cheaper are available.

On the supply side, many households simply live in rural areas or urban neighborhoods that do not have access to piped water. In addition, even when there is access somewhere in the neighborhood, many households may still live too far from the network to have an opportunity to connect. Even if some households would like to connect, there may be a lack of capacity within the utility company to provide such connections, for example due to lack of workforce or other resources, or simply because production capacity is too low. In some cases, a policy may be in place in the utility company not to extend the network, because the utility already faces capacity constraints to properly serve existing consumers. In many sub-Saharan countries, water cuts are frequent, as the production and distribution capacity of utilities is limited and insufficient to meet the existing demand. There may also be financial factors affecting the capacity or willingness of the utilities to expand their network, especially if tariffs and fees are too low to permit cost recovery.

As noted among by a number of authors (Estache, Foster, and Wodon 2002; Komives et al. 2005; Estache and Wodon 2014), the policies that need to be implemented in order to promote higher coverage rates are very different depending on the nature of the obstacles to increase coverage. If the main obstacle is low demand due to a lack of affordability, utilities or governments may consider implementing special tariffs or subsidies for the poor, whether this is done for reducing the cost of the consumption of households once they are connected or for reducing the cost of connecting itself. If the main problem is low supply, the first line of answer lies in finding the necessary resources in order to strengthen the network—whether in terms of production or distribution, in order to better reach those who do not have access. Given that the policy options for dealing with demand as opposed to supply-side constraints are fairly different, it is important to try to measure the contributions of both demand- and supply-side factors to low coverage of infrastructure services. The aim of this chapter is to show how this can be done empirically in a simple way using household survey data for Uganda.

The importance of assessing the role of demand as opposed to supply-side factors in basic infrastructure coverage has been recognized among others by Foster and Araujo (2004; hereafter F&A) in their study of the impact of infrastructure reforms on the poor in Guatemala. These authors proposed a simple statistical method for assessing the contribution of pure demand-side problems, pure supply-side problems, and combined demand- and supply-side problems to coverage deficits. If a household living in an area with access to a network service was not connected, this was taken as a sign that the service was not affordable for the household (pure demand-side problem). In practice, the authors assessed whether households lived in an area with access simply by checking if any other household living in the same primary sampling unit of the survey had access. This can be done with household surveys since survey samples rely on geographically defined primary sampling units, which tend to be well-delimited areas. To the extent that the primary sampling units are not too large, access by one household in the primary sampling unit could be considered as indicating potential access for all the households in that primary sampling unit.

F&A then defined the magnitude of supply-side problems as the part of the lack of coverage that was not due to the pure demand-side problem. In addition, they decomposed supply-side problems into two components. The authors noted that even if there were access to the service in neighborhoods currently without access, some households would still not connect to the network. They argued that in areas without access, there was for some households a combined lack of demand and supply. For those households who would probably connect to the network if there were access in their neighborhood to the service, the authors argued that there was a genuine pure supply-side problem. Overall, the authors thus decomposed the lack of coverage of the network in the sum of a pure demand-side problem, a pure supply-side problem, and a combined demand- and supply-side problems. Others, including Angel-Urdinola, Cosgrove-Davies, and Wodon (2006), Angel-Urdinola and Wodon (2007, 2012), and Komives et al. (2005, 2007), have expanded on the work of F&A in order to analyze factors determining not only who connects or not to the network but also who benefits (or is likely to benefit) from various utility subsidies.

However, a weakness with the simple statistical approach used by F&A lies in the fact that there are limitations in the surveys used to assess empirically the magnitude of demand-side and supply-side problems, and that this may lead to biases in the estimates of demand as opposed to supply-side problems. Some households may live in an area where there is access to the service, but may still be located too far from the network to be able to connect (or perhaps the capacity of the network to support more households is limited). Under the simple empirical procedure for estimating demand-side and supply-side problems proposed by F&A, these households would be considered as suffering from a demand-side problem, while the true nature of the issue may be a supply-side constraint. To some extent, this type of biases can be dealt with by using regression techniques, as shown by Wodon et al. (2009). The objective of this chapter is to apply the Wodon et al. (2009) methodology to piped water coverage in Uganda and compare the results obtained with those from the F&A approach.

The chapter is structured as follows. In section 2, we describe the approach used by F&A for assessing the relative role of demand- and supply-side problems to account for the lack of coverage of modern infrastructure services. That section also presents the alternative econometric approach proposed by Wodon et al. (2009). The results obtained with both approaches for Uganda are then provided in section 3. A conclusion follows.

Methodology

In this chapter, we look at whether the main barrier to higher connection rates among households not connected to the network (this could be for piped water or electricity, for example) is likely to be due to demand- or supply-side factors. We start by presenting in mathematical notation the approach proposed by F&A (2004) for assessing demand- and supply-side problems limiting coverage of network services and continue with the method proposed by Wodon et al. (2009) to improve on such assessments.

Coverage rate is defined as the product of the access rate in a neighborhood (A) and the take-up or uptake (U) rates where access is available (C = A × U). The share of the population not served by the network is 1–C. The objective is to assess whether the unserved population is not served due to a demand-side problem (the service is available, but not taken up by the households, probably because it is not affordable, but perhaps also because it is of low quality) or a supply-side problem (the service is simply not available to households). F&A (2004) define the pure demand-side gap (PDSG) as follows:

$$PDSG = A - C = A \times (1 - U)$$

This definition implies that when there is access in the area where a household lives, if a household does not take-up the service, it is symptomatic of a demand issue. Thus, lack of demand is responsible for all of the difference between the neighborhood access rate A and the actual coverage rate C. Next, the authors define the supply-side gap as follows:

$$SSG = (1 - C) - PDSG = (1 - A \times U) - A \times (1 - U) = 1 - A$$

In other words, the supply gap is the difference between the neighborhood access rate and the coverage rate. Said differently, the sum of the pure demand-side gap, the supply-side gap, and the coverage rate is equal to one:

$$PDSG + SSG + C = 1$$

However, in areas that are not covered by the network and which are responsible for the supply gap above, it is likely that even if supply were available, some households would not take up the service due to affordability issues. If one assumes that the take-up rate in nonserved areas would be similar to the take-up rate in areas where there is service now, the additional coverage that we would obtain by providing access to these areas would be equal to the supply-side gap times the take-up rate where there is access. This is defined as the pure supply-side gap:

$$PSSG = SSG \times U = (1 - A) \times U$$

The difference between the pure supply-side gap and the supply-side gap can then be deemed to represent a combined demand- and supply-side gaps, since first there is no access to the service, and second even if there were access, some households would not be connected. F&A defined this as the mixed demand- and supply-side gaps, defined as follows:

$$MDSSG = SSG \times (1 - U)$$

Given the above definitions, the proportion of the deficit in coverage that is attributed to demand-side factors is defined as the ratio of the pure demand-side gap to the unserved population. The proportion of deficit attributable to supply-side factors is the ratio of the pure supply-side gap divided by the unserved population. Finally, the proportion of deficit attributable to both demand- and supply-side factors is the ratio of the mixed demand- and supply-side gaps divided by the unserved population. The sum of the three proportions is equal to one.

A weakness of this statistical approach is that all households not connecting to the network where there is access are assumed to suffer from a demand-side problem, which may lead to an overestimation of the proportion of deficit coverage that is attributed to demand-side factors. Wodon et al. (2009) proposed an alternative econometric method to try to better identify demand- and supply-side problems. Their method is used here. We estimate a regression of the determinants of the take-up of the household as a function of the following variables: a set of dummies for the quintile of well-being to which the household belongs, and the leave-out mean take-up rate in the primary sampling unit where the household lives. In the case of Uganda, since we have consumption data, that is the variable used to assess welfare.

The regressions on take-up of service are estimated only on the samples of households that live in neighborhoods where there is access at the neighborhood level, and the estimation follows a simple probit procedure. The regressions are not presented here, as there are many of them, but they are rather straightforward. The leave-out mean access rate is meant to capture the general conditions of the neighborhood (including factors such as the average distance from the electric network), while the quintiles of welfare are used to deal with the affordability issue.

Once the regressions have been estimated, we simulate what the access rate would be if all households living in areas where there is access would be lifted in terms of well-being from wherever they are in the distribution of well-being to the top quintile of well-being. That is, we simulate what the take-up rate would be for all households living in primary sampling units where there is access based on what the behavior of the households would be if they were in the top quintile, which corresponds implicitly to an assumption of no affordability problem, since the households in the top quintile should be able to afford piped water services.

Residential Piped Water in Uganda · http://dx.doi.org/10.1596/978-1-4648-0708-4

When aggregating the results for an area as a whole, we denote by U^* the alternative take-up rate obtained in this way ($U^* > U$). We then define the adjusted pure demand-side gap ($APDSG$) as follows:

$$APDSG = A \times (U^* - U)$$

This definition means that we consider as a demand-side or affordability issues the difference between the observed take-up rate and the simulated take-up rate when all households are given the wealth of the richest households in the country. We next define the adjusted supply-side gap as follows:

$$ASSG = (1 - C) - APDSG = (1 - A \times U) - A \times (U^* - U) = 1 - AU^*$$

The adjusted supply-side gap is thus the difference between full coverage and the coverage that would be achieved taking into account first the current level of availability of the network in areas (the A variable), and second the take-up rate expected when there is no affordability issue. As before, the sum of the adjusted pure demand-side gap, the adjusted supply-side gap, and the coverage rate is equal to one:

$$APDSG + ASSG + C = 1$$

The third step is to decompose the adjusted supply-side gap into two components. First, the adjusted pure supply-side gap is defined as follows:

$$APSSG = ASSG \times U^* = (1 - AU^*) \times U^*$$

Finally, the adjusted mixed demand and supply-side gap is defined as follows:

$$AMDSSG = ASSG \times (1 - U^*) = (1 - AU^*) \times U^*$$

The proportions of the deficit in coverage due to demand-side, supply-side, and combined problems can then be computed using the above adjusted definitions, with the sum of the three proportions still being equal to one.

Empirical Results

The estimations using both the statistical and econometric approaches are implemented with the Uganda National Household Surveys for 2009/10 and 2012/13. The use of two different surveys for the analysis is useful to ensure robustness of the findings, which should turn out similar in both years, given that access, take-up, and coverage rates have not changes substantially between the two years. The results from the estimations carried with both the F&A (2004) method and the alternative proposed by Wodon et al. (2009) are provided in tables 3.1 and 3.2 for the 2009/10 survey, and in tables 3.3 and 3.4 for the

Table 3.1 Statistical Estimation of Demand- and Supply-side Constraints to Coverage (F&A approach), 2009/10

Percent

	Access	Take-up	Coverage	Unserved population	Pure demand-side gap	Supply-side gap	Pure supply side-gap	Mixed demand-and supply-side gaps	Proportion of deficit attributable to demand-side factors only	Proportion of deficit attributable to supply-side factors only	Proportion of deficit attributable to both supply-and demand-side factors
Uganda											
National	19.1	26.8	5.1	94.9	13.9	80.9	21.7	59.3	14.7	22.9	62.4
Urban	69.2	28.5	19.7	80.3	49.4	30.8	8.8	22.0	61.6	11.0	27.4
Rural	7.4	23.0	1.7	98.3	5.7	92.6	21.3	71.3	5.8	21.7	72.5
Region											
Central	39.1	27.6	10.8	89.2	28.3	60.9	16.8	44.0	31.8	18.9	49.4
Eastern	7.8	25.6	2.0	98.0	5.8	92.2	23.6	68.6	5.9	24.1	70.0
Northern	9.2	21.2	1.9	98.1	7.2	90.8	19.2	71.6	7.4	19.6	73.0
Western	12.8	27.4	3.5	96.5	9.3	87.2	23.9	63.3	9.6	24.8	65.6
Stratum											
Kampala	72.5	29.5	21.4	78.6	51.1	27.5	8.1	19.4	65.1	10.3	24.6
Central 1	37.2	30.7	11.4	88.6	25.8	62.8	19.3	43.5	29.1	21.7	49.1
Central 2	21.2	17.7	3.7	96.3	17.4	78.8	13.9	64.9	18.1	14.5	67.4
East Central	9.3	27.6	2.6	97.4	6.7	90.7	25.0	65.6	6.9	25.7	67.4
Eastern	6.6	23.4	1.6	98.4	5.1	93.4	21.9	71.5	5.1	22.2	72.6
Mid-Northern	8.8	14.4	1.3	98.7	7.5	91.2	13.2	78.0	7.6	13.4	79.0
North-East	4.7	21.0	1.0	99.0	3.7	95.3	20.1	75.3	3.7	20.3	76.0
West-Nile	12.0	27.8	3.3	96.7	8.6	88.0	24.4	63.6	8.9	25.3	65.8
Mid-Western	11.9	17.6	2.1	97.9	9.8	88.1	15.5	72.6	10.0	15.9	74.1
South-Western	13.5	35.1	4.8	95.2	8.8	86.5	30.4	56.1	9.2	31.9	58.9

table continues next page

Table 3.1 Statistical Estimation of Demand- and Supply-side Constraints to Coverage (F&A approach), 2009/10 *(continued)*

	Access	Take-up	Coverage	Unserved population	Pure demand-side gap	Supply-side gap	Pure supply side-gap	Mixed demand- and supply-side gaps	Proportion of deficit attributable to demand-side factors only	Proportion of deficit attributable to supply-side factors only	Proportion of deficit attributable to both supply- and demand-side factors
Region urban/rural											
Central rural	16.5	22.5	3.7	96.3	12.8	83.5	18.8	64.7	13.3	19.5	67.2
Central urban	76.1	29.4	22.4	77.6	53.7	23.9	7.0	16.8	69.2	9.1	21.7
East rural	4.0	23.1	0.9	99.1	3.1	96.0	22.2	73.8	3.1	22.4	74.4
East urban	42.5	27.8	11.8	88.2	30.7	57.5	16.0	41.5	34.8	18.1	47.1
North rural	5.2	18.8	1.0	99.0	4.2	94.8	17.8	77.0	4.3	18.0	77.7
North urban	45.3	23.7	10.7	89.3	34.5	54.7	13.0	41.8	38.7	14.5	46.8
West rural	4.6	28.3	1.3	98.7	3.3	95.4	27.0	68.3	3.4	27.4	69.2
West urban	81.0	27.0	21.8	78.2	59.2	19.0	5.1	13.8	75.7	6.5	17.7

Source: Data from 2009/10 UNHS survey. All variables are expressed as percentages (%).

34

Table 3.2 Econometric Estimation of Demand- and Supply-side Constraints to Coverage (Wodon et al. Approach), 2009/10

Percent

	Access	Take-up	Adjusted take-up rate given access	Coverage	Unserved population	Adjusted pure demand-side gap	Adjusted supply-side gap	Adjusted pure supply side gap	Adjusted mixed demand- and supply-side gaps	Adjusted proportion of deficit attributable to demand-side factors only	Adjusted proportion of deficit attributable to supply-side factors only	Adjusted proportion of deficit attributable to both supply- and demand-side factors
Uganda												
National	19.1	26.8	34.8	5.1	94.9	1.5	93.4	32.5	60.9	1.6	34.2	64.2
Urban	69.2	28.5	34.7	19.7	80.3	4.3	76.0	26.4	49.6	5.3	32.9	61.8
Rural	7.4	23.0	36.7	1.7	98.3	1.0	97.3	35.7	61.5	1.0	36.4	62.6
Region												
Central	39.1	27.6	34.2	10.8	89.2	2.6	86.6	29.6	57.0	2.9	33.2	63.9
Eastern	7.8	25.6	41.3	2.0	98.0	1.2	96.8	39.9	56.9	1.2	40.7	58.0
Northern	9.2	21.2	32.7	1.9	98.1	1.1	97.0	31.7	65.3	1.1	32.4	66.6
Western	12.8	27.4	37.8	3.5	96.5	1.3	95.2	36.0	59.2	1.4	37.3	61.4
Stratum												
Kampala	72.5	29.5	33.5	21.4	78.6	2.9	75.7	25.4	50.3	3.7	32.3	64.0
Central 1	37.2	30.7	42.3	11.4	88.6	4.3	84.3	35.6	48.6	4.9	40.2	54.9
Central 2	21.2	17.7	28.8	3.7	96.3	2.4	93.9	27.1	66.8	2.5	28.1	69.4
East Central	9.3	27.6	36.8	2.6	97.4	0.9	96.6	35.5	61.0	0.9	36.5	62.6
Eastern	6.6	23.4	52.0	1.6	98.4	1.9	96.6	50.2	46.4	1.9	51.0	47.1
Mid-Northern	8.8	14.4	29.1	1.3	98.7	1.3	97.4	28.4	69.1	1.3	28.7	70.0
North-East	4.7	21.0	25.0	1.0	99.0	0.2	98.8	24.7	74.1	0.2	24.9	74.9
West-Nile	12.0	27.8	38.9	3.3	96.7	1.3	95.3	37.1	58.2	1.4	38.4	60.2
Mid-Western	11.9	17.6	33.4	2.1	97.9	1.9	96.0	32.1	63.9	1.9	32.8	65.3
South-Western	13.5	35.1	39.2	4.8	95.2	0.5	94.7	37.1	57.6	0.6	38.9	60.5

table continues next page

Table 3.2 Econometric Estimation of Demand- and Supply-side Constraints to Coverage (Wodon et al. Approach), 2009/10 (continued)

Region urban/rural	Access	Take-up	Adjusted take-up rate given access	Coverage	Unserved population	Adjusted pure demand-side gap	Adjusted supply-side gap	Adjusted pure supply-side gap	Adjusted mixed demand- and supply-side gaps	Adjusted proportion of deficit attributable to demand-side factors only	Adjusted proportion of deficit attributable to supply-side factors only	Adjusted proportion of deficit attributable to both supply- and demand-side factors
Central rural	16.5	22.5	32.3	3.7	96.3	1.6	94.7	30.6	64.1	1.7	31.7	66.6
Central urban	76.1	29.4	35.0	22.4	77.6	4.3	73.3	25.7	47.6	5.5	33.1	61.4
East rural	4.0	23.1	55.5	0.9	99.1	1.3	97.8	54.3	43.5	1.3	54.8	43.9
East urban	42.5	27.8	32.9	11.8	88.2	2.2	86.0	28.3	57.7	2.5	32.1	65.4
North rural	5.2	18.8	34.6	1.0	99.0	0.8	98.2	34.0	64.2	0.8	34.3	64.9
North urban	45.3	23.7	35.1	10.7	89.3	5.2	84.1	29.6	54.5	5.8	33.1	61.1
West rural	4.6	28.3	47.2	1.3	98.7	0.9	97.8	46.1	51.7	0.9	46.8	52.4
West urban	81.0	27.0	34.1	21.8	78.2	5.8	72.4	24.7	47.7	7.4	31.6	61.0

Source: Data from 2009/10 UNHS survey. All variables are expressed as percentages (%).

Table 3.3 Statistical Estimation of Demand- and Supply-side Constraints to Coverage (F&A approach), 2012/13

Percent

	Access	Take-up	Coverage	Unserved population	Pure demand-side gap	Supply-side gap	Pure supply-side gap	Mixed demand- and supply-side gaps	Proportion of deficit attributable to demand-side factors only	Proportion of deficit attributable to supply-side factors only	Proportion of deficit attributable to both supply- and demand-side factors
Uganda											
National	20.0	35.2	7.0	93.0	12.9	80.0	28.2	51.9	13.9	30.3	55.8
Urban	59.5	38.4	22.8	77.2	36.6	40.5	15.6	25.0	47.5	20.2	32.4
Rural	5.6	22.8	1.3	98.7	4.3	94.4	21.5	72.9	4.4	21.8	73.8
Region											
Central	35.8	38.9	14.0	86.0	21.9	64.2	25.0	39.2	25.4	29.0	45.5
Eastern	12.0	34.7	4.2	95.8	7.8	88.0	30.6	57.5	8.2	31.9	60.0
Northern	7.5	18.6	1.4	98.6	6.1	92.5	17.2	75.4	6.2	17.4	76.4
Western	19.6	32.5	6.4	93.6	13.3	80.4	26.1	54.3	14.2	27.9	58.0
Stratum											
Kampala	94.2	48.6	45.8	54.2	48.4	5.8	2.8	3.0	89.3	5.2	5.5
Central 1	25.3	28.5	7.2	92.8	18.1	74.7	21.3	53.4	19.5	23.0	57.6
Central 2	22.3	34.7	7.7	92.3	14.5	77.7	27.0	50.8	15.8	29.2	55.0
East Central	15.4	39.2	6.0	94.0	9.3	84.6	33.2	51.4	9.9	35.3	54.7
Eastern	9.5	29.3	2.8	97.2	6.7	90.5	26.5	64.0	6.9	27.3	65.8
Mid-Northern	7.1	17.8	1.3	98.7	5.8	92.9	16.5	76.4	5.9	16.8	77.4
North-East	1.9	22.7	0.4	99.6	1.5	98.1	22.3	75.8	1.5	22.4	76.1
West-Nile	10.6	19.1	2.0	98.0	8.6	89.4	17.0	72.4	8.7	17.4	73.9
Mid-Western	12.5	41.9	5.2	94.8	7.3	87.5	36.7	50.9	7.7	38.7	53.7
South-Western	26.3	28.3	7.4	92.6	18.8	73.7	20.9	52.9	20.3	22.6	57.1

table continues next page

Table 3.3 Statistical Estimation of Demand- and Supply-side Constraints to Coverage (F&A approach), 2012/13 *(continued)*

	Access	Take-up	Coverage	Unserved population	Pure demand-side gap	Supply-side gap	Pure supply-side gap	Mixed demand- and supply-side gaps	Proportion of deficit attributable to demand-side factors only	Proportion of deficit attributable to supply-side factors only	Proportion of deficit attributable to both supply- and demand-side factors
Region urban/rural											
Central rural	5.6	19.1	1.1	98.9	4.5	94.4	18.0	76.4	4.6	18.2	77.2
Central urban	73.4	40.8	30.0	70.0	43.4	26.6	10.9	15.7	62.0	15.5	22.5
East rural	3.6	20.1	0.7	99.3	2.9	96.4	19.4	77.0	2.9	19.5	77.5
East urban	50.5	39.6	20.0	80.0	30.5	49.5	19.6	29.9	38.1	24.5	37.4
North rural	2.9	21.5	0.6	99.4	2.2	97.1	20.9	76.2	2.3	21.0	76.7
North urban	29.7	17.2	5.1	94.9	24.6	70.3	12.1	58.2	25.9	12.7	61.4
West rural	10.3	26.1	2.7	97.3	7.6	89.7	23.4	66.3	7.8	24.1	68.1
West urban	52.1	36.8	19.2	80.8	32.9	47.9	17.7	30.3	40.7	21.8	37.5

Source: Data from 2012/13 UNHS survey. All variables are expressed as percentages (%).

Table 3.4 Econometric Estimation of Demand- and Supply-side Constraints to Coverage (Wodon et al. Approach), 2012/13

Percent

	Access	Take-up	Adjusted Take-up rate given access	Coverage	Unserved population	Adjusted pure demand-side gap	Adjusted supply-side gap	Adjusted pure supply-side gap	Adjusted mixed demand- and supply-side gaps	Adjusted proportion of deficit attributable to demand-side factors only	Adjusted proportion of deficit attributable to supply-side factors only	Adjusted proportion of deficit attributable to both supply- and demand-side factors
Uganda												
National	20.0	35.2	44.8	7.0	93.0	1.9	91.1	40.8	50.2	2.1	43.9	54.0
Urban	59.5	38.4	46.8	22.8	77.2	5.0	72.2	33.8	38.4	6.4	43.8	49.8
Rural	5.6	22.8	37.0	1.3	98.7	0.8	97.9	36.3	61.7	0.8	36.8	62.4
Region												
Central	35.8	38.9	47.3	14.0	86.0	3.0	83.0	39.3	43.7	3.5	45.7	50.8
Eastern	12.0	34.7	46.8	4.2	95.8	1.4	94.4	44.2	50.2	1.5	46.1	52.4
Northern	7.5	18.6	28.2	1.4	98.6	0.7	97.9	27.6	70.3	0.7	28.0	71.3
Western	19.6	32.5	42.1	6.4	93.6	1.9	91.7	38.6	53.2	2.0	41.2	56.8
Stratum												
Kampala	94.2	48.6	53.6	45.8	54.2	4.7	49.5	26.5	23.0	8.6	49.0	42.4
Central 1	25.3	28.5	37.8	7.2	92.8	2.4	90.4	34.2	56.2	2.5	36.9	60.6
Central 2	22.3	34.7	43.5	7.7	92.3	2.0	90.3	39.3	51.1	2.1	42.5	55.3
East Central	15.4	39.2	49.2	6.0	94.0	1.5	92.4	45.5	46.9	1.6	48.4	50.0
Eastern	9.5	29.3	44.0	2.8	97.2	1.4	95.8	42.2	53.7	1.4	43.4	55.2
Mid-Northern	7.1	17.8	26.3	1.3	98.7	0.6	98.1	25.8	72.3	0.6	26.1	73.2
North-East	1.9	22.7	n.a.	0.4	99.6	n.a.	n.a.	n.a.	n.a.	n.a.	n.a.	n.a.
West-Nile	10.6	19.1	27.6	2.0	98.0	0.9	97.1	26.8	70.3	0.9	27.4	71.7
Mid-Western	12.5	41.9	46.1	5.2	94.8	0.5	94.2	43.4	50.8	0.6	45.8	53.6
South-Western	26.3	28.3	41.1	7.4	92.6	3.3	89.2	36.6	52.6	3.6	39.6	56.8

table continues next page

Table 3.4 Econometric Estimation of Demand- and Supply-side Constraints to Coverage (Wodon et al. Approach), 2012/13 (continued)

	Access	Take-up	Adjusted Take-up rate given access	Coverage	Unserved population	Adjusted pure demand-side gap	Adjusted supply-side gap	Adjusted pure supply-side gap	Adjusted mixed demand- and supply-side gaps	Adjusted proportion of deficit attributable to demand-side factors only	Adjusted proportion of deficit attributable to supply-side factors only	Adjusted proportion of deficit attributable to both supply- and demand-side factors
Region urban/rural												
Central rural	5.6	19.1	31.8	1.1	98.9	0.7	98.2	31.2	67.0	0.7	31.6	67.7
Central urban	73.4	40.8	48.6	30.0	70.0	5.7	64.3	31.3	33.1	8.1	44.6	47.2
East rural	3.6	20.1	35.8	0.7	99.3	0.6	98.7	35.3	63.4	0.6	35.6	63.8
East urban	50.5	39.6	49.8	20.0	80.0	5.2	74.9	37.3	37.6	6.5	46.6	47.0
North rural	2.9	21.5	38.9	0.6	99.4	0.5	98.9	38.5	60.4	0.5	38.7	60.8
North urban	29.7	17.2	22.6	5.1	94.9	1.6	93.3	21.1	72.2	1.7	22.2	76.1
West rural	10.3	26.1	39.1	2.7	97.3	1.3	96.0	37.5	58.5	1.4	38.5	60.1
West urban	52.1	36.8	44.1	19.2	80.8	3.8	77.0	34.0	43.1	4.7	42.0	53.3

Source: Data from 2012/13 UNHS survey. All variables are expressed as percentages (%).

Note: n.a. = not applicable. For the Mid-Northern stratum and the North rural region, the estimations did not provide appropriate results due to limited sample size with coverage.

2012/13 survey. In those tables, results are also provided by region (Central, Eastern, Northern, and Western), stratum in the surveys (Kampala, Central 1, Central 2, East Central, Eastern, Mid-Northern, North-East, West-Nile, Mid-Western, South-Western), and finally by urban and rural areas in each of the four regions.

Summary results nationally and for urban and rural areas are provided in table 3.5. The results obtained with both the statistical and econometric approaches are very similar in the two years, as expected. Consider the results for 2012/13. In the statistical approach, demand-side factors account for 13.9 percent of the coverage gap at the national level, while supply-side factors account for 30.3 percent of the gap. The rest of the coverage gap (55.8 percent) is due to combined demand- and supply-side factors. With the econometric approach, supply-side factors account for a larger share of the gap (43.9 percent), with combined factors accounting for 54 percent of the gap and demand-side factors for the rest (only 2.1 percent). The results in terms of the size of demand and supply factors limiting take-up change when using the econometric as opposed to the statistical approach. Similar findings are observed for urban and rural areas.

The analysis was also carried according to Ugandan's regions/areas and by urban–rural areas within regions/areas, as well as by strata. This provides a set of 22 observations. The relative importance of demand-side constraints, supply-side constraints, and combined constraints with the econometric is visualized in figure 3.1. In each panel of the figure, we have a scatter plot with the average neighborhood access rate in the region/area on the horizontal axis and the estimates from the econometric method of the proportions of the coverage deficit due respectively to demand-side factors, supply-side factors, and combined factors on the vertical axis. The curves through the scatter plots have been fitted in Excel for visual purposes.

Table 3.5 Summary Results on Demand- and Supply-side Constraints to Coverage

Percent

	2009/10			2012/13		
	Demand-side factors (%)	Supply-side factors (%)	Combined factors (%)	Demand-side factors (%)	Supply-side factors (%)	Combined factors (%)
Statistical Approach						
National	14.7	22.9	62.4	13.9	30.3	55.8
Urban	61.6	11.0	27.4	47.5	20.2	32.4
Rural	5.8	21.7	72.5	4.4	21.8	73.8
Econometric Approach						
National	1.6	34.2	64.2	2.1	43.9	54.0
Urban	5.3	32.9	61.8	6.4	43.8	49.8
Rural	1.0	36.4	62.6	0.8	36.8	62.4

Source: Data from 2009/10 and 2012/13 UNHS surveys. All variables are expressed as percentages (%).

Residential Piped Water in Uganda • http://dx.doi.org/10.1596/978-1-4648-0708-4

Figure 3.1 Demand and Supply Constraints to Piped Water Coverage

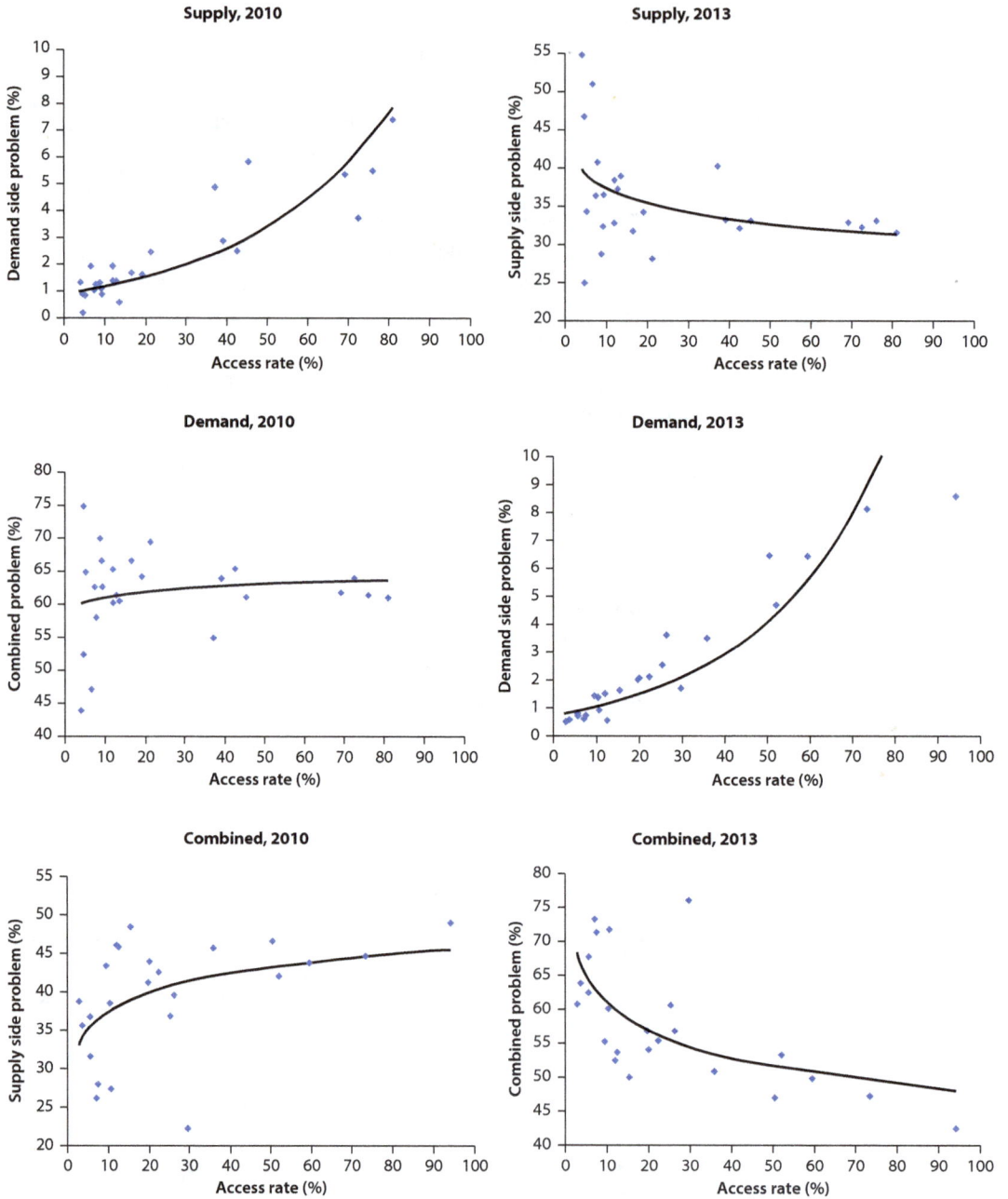

Source: Data from Uganda 2009/10 and 2012/13 surveys.

Clearly, demand-side factors are more important in areas where access is already high, as expected. Supply-side factors are less important in areas with higher access, also as expected. The relationship between combined factors and access rates is less significant and depends on the year considered. Still, overall, the key conclusion from the exercise is that supply-side issues are clearly more important than demand-side issues in Uganda to explain coverage gaps. In order to provide additional visualization of the results, map 3.1 and map 3.2 provide maps of Uganda with the intensity of the shading reflecting the relative size of demand, supply, and combined factors in accounting for residential piped water

Map 3.1 Demand, Supply, and Combined Constraints According to the Statistical Approach, 2012/13

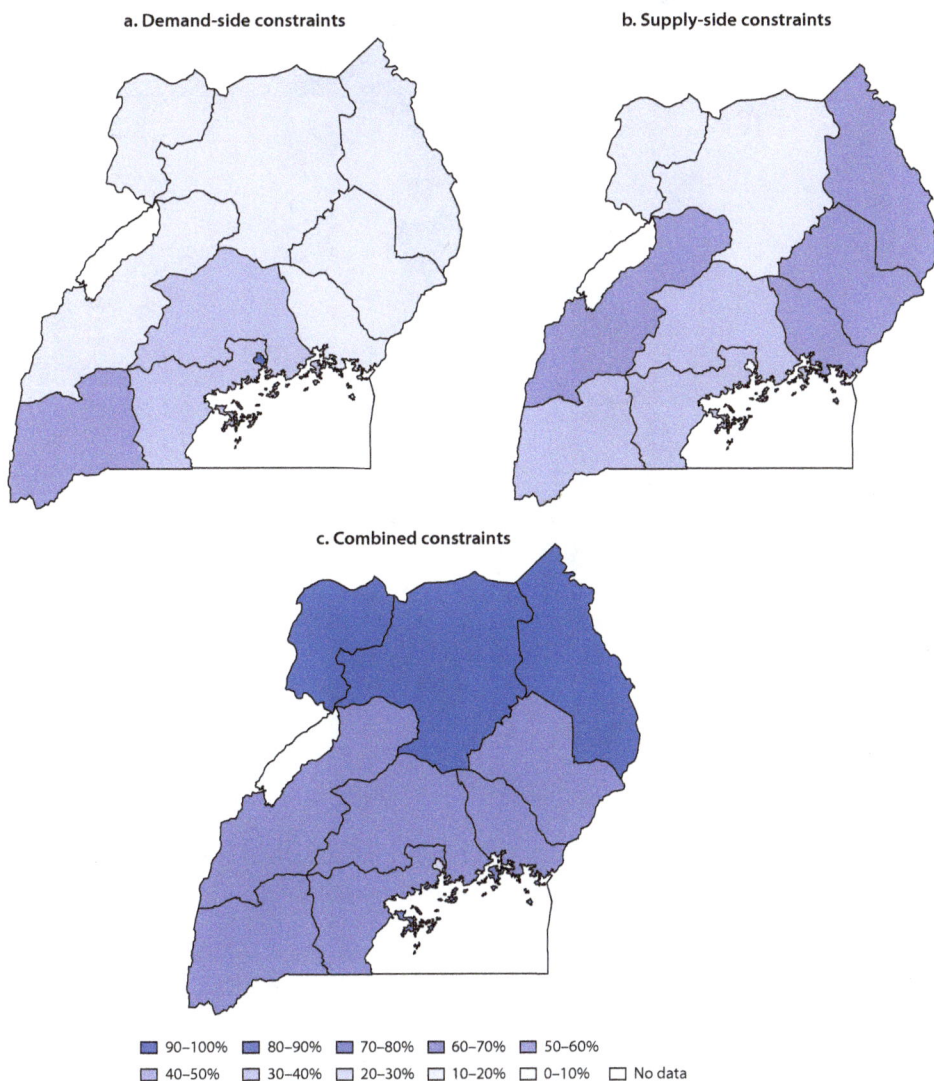

a. Demand-side constraints   b. Supply-side constraints

c. Combined constraints

90–100% 80–90% 70–80% 60–70% 50–60%
40–50% 30–40% 20–30% 10–20% 0–10% No data

Source: Data from 2012/13 UNHS survey.

Map 3.2 Demand, Supply, and Combined Constraints According to the Econometric Approach, 2012/13

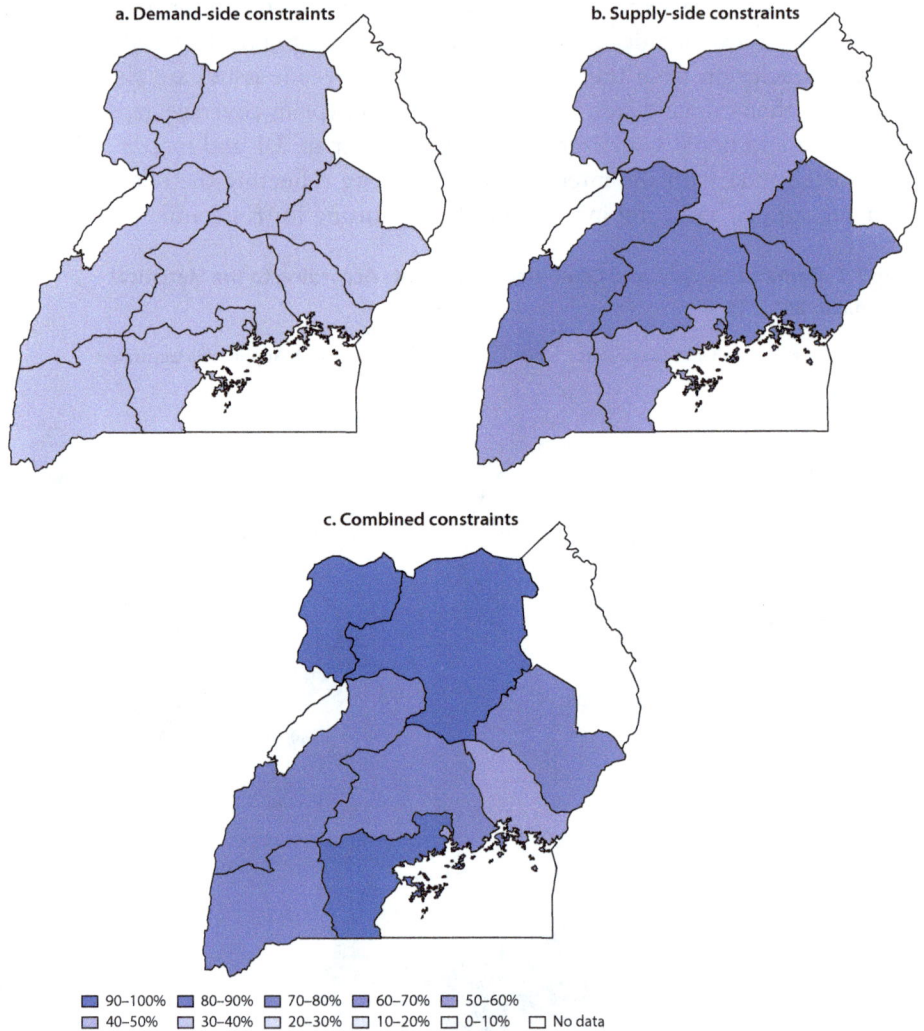

a. Demand-side constraints

b. Supply-side constraints

c. Combined constraints

■ 90–100%	■ 80–90%	■ 70–80%	■ 60–70%	■ 50–60%
■ 40–50%	■ 30–40%	■ 20–30%	□ 10–20%	□ 0–10% □ No data

Source: Data from 2012/13 UNHS survey.

coverage gap in each geographic area. This is done for the statistical approach in map 3.1 and for the econometric approach in map 3.2.

Conclusion

Many African countries are aiming to improve coverage of network-based infrastructure services such as piped water in the population. Yet, in order to inform appropriate policies to do so, it is important to first understand whether lack of coverage is due primarily to demand-side or affordability issues, to a lack of supply, or to a combination of both. Some households may live in areas where access to piped water is in principle available, but may not be able to pay for those services. Other households may be able to pay for the services, but may live too far from the network to be able to connect.

In this chapter, using the last two household surveys for Uganda, we have used two different methods for decomposing the lack of coverage observed in various areas into three components: pure demand-side constraints, pure supply-side constraints, and combined demand- and supply-side constraints. The results obtained with the statistical method suggest that demand-side constraints account for a substantial share of the coverage gap. But the results obtained from the econometric method, which is arguably more reliable, suggest that lack of supply appears to be the main issue, as one might expect in a country like Uganda.

The method used here could be refined for more detailed policy work. For example, one could check the robustness of the econometric simulations to alternative estimation techniques, or alternative specifications of the regressions. One could also rely on census data in order to obtain estimates of demand-side as opposed to supply-side constraints for smaller geographic areas. The results obtained from survey or census data could also be combined with additional information from willingness to pay studies or focus-group discussions. But overall, even though this may not be too surprising for Uganda, it is useful to know that the data confirm the prominence of supply over demand constraints in explaining low coverage rates in the country.

References

Angel-Urdinola, D., M. Cosgrove-Davies, and Q. Wodon. 2006. "Rwanda: Piped Water Tariff Reform." In *Poverty and Social Impact Analysis of Reforms Lessons and Examples from Implementation*, edited by A. Coudouel, A. Dani, and S. Paternostro. Washington, DC: World Bank.

Angel-Urdinola, D., and Q. Wodon. 2007. "Do Utility Subsidies Reach the Poor? Framework and Evidence for Cape Verde, Sao Tome, and Rwanda." *Economics Bulletin* 9 (4): 1–7.

———. 2012. "Does Increasing Access to Infrastructure Services Improve the Targeting Performance of Water Subsidies?" *Journal of International Development* 24 (1): 88–101.

Banerjee, S., Q. Wodon, A. Diallo, and V. Foster. 2009. "Trends in Household Coverage of Modern Infrastructure Services in Africa." Policy Research Working Paper No. 4880, World Bank, Washington, DC.

Banerjee, S., Q. Wodon, A. Diallo, T. Pushak, H. Uddin, C. Tsimpo, and V. Foster 2008. "Access, Affordability and Alternatives: Modern Infrastructure Services in Africa." Africa Infrastructure Country Diagnostic Study Background Paper 2, World Bank, Washington, DC.

Banerjee, S., Q. Wodon, and V. Foster. 2010. "Dealing with Poverty and Inequality." In *Africa's Infrastructure: A Time for Transformation*, edited by V. Foster and C. Briceno-

Garmendia. Washington, DC: Africa Development Forum, Agence Française de Développement and World Bank.

Clarke, R. G., and S. J. Wallsten. 2003. "Universal Service: Empirical Evidence on the Provision of Infrastructure Services to Rural and Poor Urban Consumers." In *Infrastructure for Poor People: Public Policy for Private Provision*, edited by P. Brook and T. Irwin. Washington, DC: World Bank.

Estache, A., V. Foster, and Q. Wodon. 2002. *Accounting for Poverty in Infrastructure Reform*. Washington, DC: World Bank.

Estache, A., and Q. Wodon. 2014. *Infrastructure and Poverty in Sub-Saharan Africa*. New York: Palgrave Macmillan.

Foster, V., and M. C. Araujo. 2004. "Does Infrastructure Reform Work for the Poor? A Case Study from Guatemala." Policy Research Working Paper 3185, World Bank, Washington, DC.

Foster, V., and C. Briceno-Garmendia, eds. 2010. *Africa's Infrastructure: A Time for Transformation*. Washington, DC: Africa Development Forum, Agence Française de Développement and World Bank.

Komives, K., V. Foster, J. Halpern, and Q. Wodon. 2005. *Water, Piped Water, and the Poor: Who Benefits from Utility Subsidies?* Directions in Development. Washington, DC: World Bank.

Komives, K., J. Halpern, V. Foster, Q. Wodon, and R. Abdullah. 2007. "Utility Subsidies as Social Transfers: An Empirical Evaluation of Targeting Performance." *Development Policy Review* 25 (6): 659–79.

Komives, K. D., M. Whittington, and X. Wu. 2003. "Infrastructure Coverage and the Poor: A Global Perspective." In *Infrastructure for Poor People: Public Policy for Private Provision*, edited by P. Brook and T. Irwin. Washington, DC: World Bank.

Mawejje, J., E. Munyambonera, and L. Bategeka. 2012. "Uganda's Piped Water Reforms and Institutional Restructuring." Economic Policy Research Centre Working Paper No. 89, Economic Policy Research Centre, Kampala.

Ranganathan, R., and V. Foster. 2012. "Uganda's Infrastructure: A Continental Perspective." World Bank Policy Research Working Paper No. 5963, World Bank, Washington, DC.

Wodon, Q., S. Banerjee, A. Diallo, and V. Foster. 2009. "Is Low Coverage of Modern Infrastructure Services in African Cities Due to Lack of Demand or Lack of Supply?" Policy Research Working Paper No. 4881, World Bank, Washington, DC.

CHAPTER 4

Piped Water Coverage, Time Use, and Poverty

Clarence Tsimpo, Quentin Wodon, Faisal Buyinza, and Willy Kagarura

Introduction

What are the benefits for households from a connection to the water network? This chapter considers one such benefit, looking at time use and its impact on household welfare. Using the last round of the Uganda National Household Survey for 2012/13, the chapter estimates the impact of a connection to the water network on domestic and productive work time. Simulations are provided about the gains in welfare and the reduction in poverty that might be generated from an expansion of network coverage. The results suggests that in areas where the network is available, a connection for households not yet connected may enable women to reduce domestic work and increase market work by about 1.5 hours and is likely to reduce poverty by up to one percentage point.

The way people allocate their time matters for productivity, poverty reduction, and economic growth. Women and children may spend considerable time on collecting water and fuel to meet domestic needs (Blackden and Wodon 2006). Hours spent on these chores are not necessarily productive and take time away from more productive activities such as acquiring human capital or working in the labor market or on the household farm. Therefore, the availability of electricity and network (piped) water may help in reducing time spent on domestic chores, and increase economic opportunities and earnings, especially for women, ultimately reducing poverty.

Time use decisions depend on household structure. Illahi (2000) notes that the presence of young children significantly affects women's time use as they withdraw from labor markets or reduce the amount of time they work outside their homes. With other adult female members in a household, the time each one must allocate to domestic work is reduced and the likelihood of participating in market work is increased. But time allocations also depend on the availability of basic infrastructure services and the impact of such services on time use can be substantial. In Kenya, Whittington, Mu, and Roche (1990) note that the time household members spend collecting water amounts to the wage rate of an unskilled worker. Ilahi and Grimard (2000) show that lack of access to water reduces the time that women devote to market work and increases their total work time. Water provision encourages a move toward market work among women and increases time available for leisure. In South Africa, Dinkelman (2008) suggests that electricity roll-outs increase women's employment rate by 14 points, whereas men's employment was not significantly affected. Grogan and Sadanand (2008) show that women's earnings increased by 60 percent in Guatemala with improved access to electricity thanks to an increase in market work. Availability of basic infrastructure may also benefit children since many spend hours fetching water or collecting wood (Blackden and Wodon 2006).

Several studies (Asian Development Bank 2010; Khandker 1996; Martins 2005; World Bank 2008) point to the role of rural electrification in improving welfare, quality of life, and growth.[1] Khandker, Barnes, and Samad (2013) find that power connections have positive impacts on income, expenditures, and schooling. Electricity benefits income generation activities through business operations being able to stay open longer. A reliable supply of electricity also creates opportunities for many small entrepreneurial activities which can take place within the household, increasing its nonwage income. Srivastava and Rehman (2006) note presence of a strong negative correlation between people leaving below the poverty line and the level of electrification. Better lighting can benefit other activities, such as sewing by women, social gatherings after dark, studying by children. Access to piped water may help prevent waterborne diseases, thereby reducing risks of infant and under-five mortality as well as child malnutrition (Fay et al. 2007), and it may also reduce the cost of water provision (Bardasi and Wodon 2008). Some cooking methods also have negative effects on health and thereby productivity, with again potential gains from access to basic infrastructure. Access to basic infrastructure is likely to reduce time poverty (Bardasi and Wodon 2010), and when children and women need to walk far away from home to fetch water or wood, they may be exposed to crime risks.

This chapter estimates the extent to which piped water coverage could help household shift time from domestic to market work in Uganda. Section 2 presents basic statistics on time use. Section 3 estimates the impact of piped water on time use, and the consumption gains that connections may generate together with the resulting reduction in poverty. A conclusion follows.

Basic Statistics

The analysis is based on data from the Uganda National Household Survey (2012/13), a nationally representative survey collected by the Uganda Bureau of Statistics. The UNHS employs a two stage sampling framework, and it covers approximately 7,000 households. The socioeconomic module provides information on household sources of water, including piped water and many alternatives, from public standpipes to boreholes, among others. A household is considered as having access to piped water if the household uses piped water for drinking purposes (another way to identify households is to look at utility bills; the results are the same). The labor force questionnaire provides information on the activity status of individuals in terms of hours worked in market activities and domestic work (mostly chores). Information is available on domestic work related to fetching water, cooking, collecting firewood, and looking after or taking care of children and the elderly. Other variables of interest include information on the structure of the household, its location, its welfare status, the education level of its members.

Table 4.1 provides data on time use in terms of the number of hours allocated to different activities by different categories of individuals. Given that the simulations entail providing access to piped water to households, the estimations are conducted on households who live in an area where access is in principle feasible because other households already are connected. In those areas, some households are connected to the network, while others are not. The sample is further restricted to individuals who are working at least some time on market activities (that typically provide earnings) and domestic chores. The idea is to assess the extent to which piped water results in a shift in working hours from domestic to productive activities, and if this is the case, the extent to which this may help in reducing poverty through higher earnings. The reason to restrict the estimation to those individuals who already are working at least some time on both market and domestic activities is that it makes the estimation easier, because issues related to some individuals entering market work after getting access to infrastructure services do not need to be modelled separately. Since most adults in the household do some market and domestic work, the restriction to that sample is not problematic. Once the effect on time use of piped water (and electricity) is estimated, simulations of poverty impact can be conducted.

In table 4.1, statistics on time use are provided for the sample as a whole (again, households living where access is available), those households connected to the network, and those households not connected. Individuals from households connected to the network (or having another source of piped water) tend to have higher market working times than individuals not connected and lower domestic work time for collecting wood and fetching water. Differences in domestic work time allocated to cooking and care of children and the elderly do not differ fundamentally between those with and those without a connection, although they are slightly lower for those with piped water. Much of the domestic work is, as expected, done by women (and children) versus adult men. Women work longer hours than men. The poor tend to have less working hours, probably because of limited opportunities for productive work. None of those findings are surprising, as they have been well documented in the literature

Table 4.1 Basic Statistics on Time Use (Number of Hours per Week per Activity), 2012/13

Percent

	All households					With piped water					Without piped water				
	Market activities	Collecting firewood	Fetching water	Cooking	Children and elderly care	Market activities	Collecting firewood	Fetching water	Cooking	Children and elderly care	Market activities	Collecting firewood	Fetching water	Cooking	Children and elderly care
Gender															
Female	50.3	1.1	2.6	14.6	11.5	54.5	0.8	1.3	13.6	12.3	47.8	1.3	3.4	15.2	11.0
Male	50.9	0.9	3.1	2.8	2.2	52.3	0.4	2.0	3.9	2.3	50.2	1.1	3.6	2.2	2.1
Residence Area															
Kampala	62.1	0.1	0.8	11.5	7.0	63.1	0.0	0.3	12.6	8.7	60.8	0.1	1.3	10.3	5.0
Other urban	50.5	0.9	2.7	10.6	8.6	51.8	0.8	2.1	9.6	9.5	49.8	0.9	3.1	11.1	8.0
Rural area	42.7	2.1	4.1	11.0	9.4	47.9	1.2	1.0	12.5	10.3	41.1	2.4	5.1	10.6	9.2
Region															
Central	56.1	0.2	1.2	10.4	7.6	58.4	0.1	0.5	11.2	8.7	54.5	0.2	1.6	9.9	6.9
Eastern	46.7	2.3	5.4	10.2	10.3	48.8	1.0	3.6	8.3	8.9	45.2	3.2	6.7	11.4	11.2
Northern	45.9	0.7	2.6	12.6	9.1	49.4	0.0	0.9	12.0	14.1	44.6	0.9	3.2	12.8	7.3
Western	45.2	1.7	3.6	11.6	8.6	49.7	1.8	1.9	12.0	10.3	43.3	1.7	4.3	11.4	7.9
Welfare quintile															
Q1	37.9	2.4	3.0	9.6	6.6	18.0	0.0	7.0	7.0	0.0	38.0	2.4	3.0	9.6	6.6
Q2	41.8	2.7	4.1	11.7	7.5	40.1	0.0	3.8	15.3	5.3	41.9	2.9	4.1	11.5	7.6
Q3	42.1	2.5	5.6	10.3	8.0	48.3	1.4	5.4	7.8	5.5	40.4	2.8	5.6	11.0	8.6
Q4	49.6	1.1	3.2	11.7	10.1	51.4	1.2	2.5	10.9	10.5	48.7	1.0	3.5	12.2	9.9
Q5	54.7	0.4	1.8	10.5	8.2	55.5	0.5	0.8	11.0	9.6	54.0	0.4	2.7	10.1	7.1

table continues next page

Table 4.1 Basic Statistics on Time Use (Number of Hours per Week per Activity), 2012/13 (continued)

	All households					With piped water					Without piped water				
	Market	Collecting firewood	Fetching water	Cooking	Children and elderly care	Market	Collecting firewood	Fetching water	Cooking	Children and elderly care	Market activities	Collecting firewood	Fetching water	Cooking	Children and elderly care
Industry															
Agriculture	32.7	2.8	3.9	11.1	8.1	31.3	1.9	2.4	9.8	7.4	33.2	3.1	4.4	11.5	8.3
Mining/utilities	58.5	0.3	2.4	11.2	8.8	61.4	0.4	1.4	12.0	9.9	56.7	0.3	3.0	10.7	8.1
Manuf./Const.	45.6	0.4	0.9	2.9	16.0	58.6	0.0	1.2	7.0	36.5	36.0	0.6	0.8	0.0	1.0
Services	59.7	0.0	1.4	6.3	4.2	57.4	0.0	0.8	4.7	5.7	62.6	0.0	2.3	8.3	2.3
Public Adm.	53.6	0.0	1.0	4.3	6.3	47.9	0.0	0.3	5.0	7.6	64.0	0.0	2.2	3.1	3.8
Missing	52.4	0.7	2.2	11.9	14.3	50.1	0.0	0.3	8.5	16.2	54.6	1.4	4.0	15.2	12.4
Total	50.5	1.0	2.8	10.9	8.5	53.9	0.7	1.5	10.8	9.4	48.6	1.3	3.5	10.9	8.0

Source: Data from 2012/13 UNHS survey.

(see, for example, the country studies and reviews in Blackden and Wodon 2006). The question is the extent to which having piped water reduces domestic work and increases market work.

Econometric Analysis and Simulations

To assess the extent to which a connection to the piped water reduces domestic work and increases market work, simple regressions are estimated for the logarithm of the number of hours worked by individuals on market and domestic tasks. The independent variables include whether the household has piped water (and electricity), as well as a range of controls. The regressions are somewhat parsimonious in their specification to avoid endogeneity issues—for example, we do not include household level quintiles of welfare as independent variables because these clearly depend on the time worked by household members. The models are as follows:

$$\ln MT_i = \alpha_0 + \alpha_1 E_i + \alpha_2 PW_i + \alpha_3 HM_i + \alpha_5 HH_i + \alpha_5 CH_i + \varepsilon_i$$

$$\ln DT_i = \beta_0 + \beta_1 E_i + \beta_2 PW_i + \beta_3 HM_i + \beta_5 HH_i + \beta_5 CH_i + v_i$$

where MT_i and DT_i are the market and domestic working times for individual i, E_i and PW_i denote the access of the household to electricity and piped water, HM_i and HH_i are vectors of characteristics for the household (HH) and for the household member (HM), HC_i is a vector of location variables, and ε_i and v_i are normally distributed error terms with usual properties.

The results of the regressions are provided in table 4.2. Many of the controls are statistically significant, but the focus here is on the impact of a piped water connection on the number of hours allocated to domestic and market work by men and women. For electricity, a connection to the network reduces domestic work for men by 22 percent (albeit from a lower base than for women) and for women by 12 percent. A connection to electricity also increases market work for women by 9 percent, but the effect for men is not statistically significant. For piped water, the effects for market and domestic work are not significant for men, but there is an increase in market work hours for women even if the decrease in domestic work hours is not statistically significant. Thus, both electricity and piped water tend to increase the time allocated to market work by women. By comparing predicted working time with and without piped water on the basis of the regressions in table 4.2, it can be shown that in the case of a connection to piped water for a household previously not connected but living in an area with access, the average gain for women in market working time is 1.5 hours.

Table 4.2 Correlates of the Logarithm of Market and Domestic Work

	Domestic work		Market work	
	Men	Women	Men	Women
Access to infrastructure				
Has electricity	−0.2181***	−0.1198**	−0.0262	0.0887***
Has piped water	−0.0599	−0.0113	0.0447	0.0797**
Location (Ref.: Urban)				
Urban without Kampala	0.1272	0.1234*	−0.1108**	−0.2028***
Rural area	0.1325	0.1635**	−0.1337***	−0.2413***
Region (Ref.: Southern)				
Eastern region	0.3938***	0.4492***	−0.1970***	−0.1309***
Northern region	−0.1910***	0.2096***	−0.0773**	0.0043
Western region	−0.1650***	0.0588*	−0.0185	0.1131***
Age and Education				
Age	0.0073	0.0125*	0.0826***	0.0565***
Age squared	−0.0001	−0.0003***	−0.0011***	−0.0008***
Primary education	−0.1519**	0.0046	−0.0238	−0.0155
Secondary or higher education	−0.2765***	−0.0949***	−0.0656*	−0.0580**
Household structur				
Polygamous marriage	0.3436***	−0.1934***	−0.1987***	0.0061
Monogamously married	0.0564	−0.4863***	−0.2166***	−0.2038***
Infants aged 0-5	0.0449	0.2491***	−0.0575**	−0.0365***
Infants aged 0–5, squared	−0.0137	−0.0318***	0.0083	0.0030
Boys aged 6–17	−0.0310	−0.0276	−0.1084***	−0.0268*
Boys aged 6–17, squared	0.0076	0.0049	0.0153***	0.0050
Girls aged 6-17	−0.0230	−0.1121***	−0.0242	−0.0275*
Girls aged 6–17, squared	−0.0064	0.0124**	0.0017	0.0024
Adults aged 18-59	−0.1683***	−0.0942***	−0.0460	0.0065
Adults aged 18–59, squared	0.0237***	0.0046	0.0103**	0.0009
Seniors aged 60+	0.0036	−0.0159	0.0364*	0.0114
Seniors aged 60+, squared	−0.0023	−0.0029	−0.0003	−0.0037
Occupation				
Mining and utilities	−0.2074***	−0.1019***	0.3646***	0.2819***
Manufacture, construction	−0.3013	0.0871	0.1439	−0.0023
ICT, finance, professional services	0.0620	−0.6145***	0.4748***	0.2356*
Public administration	0.1111	−0.5033*	0.3535***	0.3523**
Missing industry	−0.1348	0.0151	0.1707*	0.0275
Constant	2.1872***	3.2628***	2.5704***	2.8103***
Observations	3,143	5,893	3,143	5,893
R-squared	0.088	0.260	0.317	0.215

Source: Estimation using Uganda UNHS 2012/13 survey.
Note: *** $p<0.01$, ** $p<0.05$, * $p<0.1$

The next step consists in estimating the potential increase in household consumption from the shift in time use away from domestic work toward market work associated with a piped water connection. The simulated counterfactual consumption level Y^C of household j is computed as follows:

$$Y_j^C = Y_j + (\Delta MT_i \times \omega_i) / N_j$$

where Y_j is the observed consumption level of the household (per equivalent adult), ΔMT_i is the increase in market working time for individual i following a connection to the network, ω_i is the expected wage or earnings of this individual (which may take the form for farm households of a higher production for household consumption), N_j is the household size (in equivalent adults), and the summation of the earnings gains is done for all working-age individuals in the household. Given the counterfactual consumption resulting from a connection to the network, denoted by Z the poverty line, by n the population in the sample (in this case, households previously not connected and which now get piped water), and by 1 the indicator function (taking a value of one if the condition is observed), the counterfactual poverty measures P^C can be estimated in a straightforward way as follows:

$$P^C = \frac{1}{n} \sum_{i=1}^{n} 1_{Z>Y_i} \left[\frac{Z - Y_i^C}{Z} \right]^\alpha$$

The headcount index of poverty is obtained for α equal to zero, the poverty gap for α equal to one, and the squared poverty gap for α equal to two. While the headcount index provides the share of the population in poverty, the poverty gap takes into account the distance separating the poor from the poverty lines as well as the proportion of the poor in the population, and the squared poverty gap is based on the square of that distance and the share in poverty. More sophisticated methods could be used to measure general equilibrium effect of the shifts in time use that take place from an piped water connection, but the estimations given in this chapter provide a quick "first round" welfare (consumption) and poverty effects from gains in working time with a connection.

A difficult question is what value to assign to ω_i, the expected gains in earnings, wages, or other benefits from working time assigned to individual i. One possibility would be to rely on the wages of individuals and to estimate wage regressions to impute wages for those who do not have a wage. The issue however is that many individuals work without wages (for example, on the household's land), so that the estimations may not be precise. An alternative is to make assumptions for likely gains in earnings based on the level of consumption of the household.

Specifically, following Bardasi and Wodon (2006), two alternative assumptions are made. In the first case, the household (as opposed to individual) earnings gain per hour of additional market work is defined as the total household consumption divided by the total working time of its members aged 14–59, including domestic time, assuming that even domestic work may help in generating earnings. In the second case, the earnings gain per hour of additional market work is obtained by dividing total household consumption by the number of hours spent by household members in market work. These two ratios can be considered a form of "household consumption productivity" because they represent the efficiency of the household in translating each hour of work (or each time of market work) by any of its member into consumption. While the first measure considers all household activities as "productive" and therefore able to generate consumption, it is true that extra-employment aimed at increasing consumption would be mostly directed at the labor market and/or in farm or family business. Therefore, in the second case only market work is considered for the denominator of the measure.

The results of the simulations are provided in table 4.3, with the base data corresponding to the actual situation of households, and the two cases corresponding to the counterfactual with the two assumptions regarding the valuation of the time essentially shifted from domestic to market work. Among households

Table 4.3 Impact on Welfare and Poverty of a Piped Water Connection

	Consumption per equivalent adult			Poverty incidence (%)			Poverty gap (%)		
		With connection			With connection			With connection	
	Base	Case 1	Case 2	Base	Case 1	Case 2	Base	Case 1	Case 2
Residence area									
Kampala	171,296	171,593	171,710	0.62	0.62	0.62	0.15	0.15	0.15
Other urban	125,049	127,023	128,418	6.13	5.58	5.23	1.35	1.18	1.01
Rural area	89,311	90,983	92,631	5.66	4.70	3.88	0.67	0.50	0.38
Region									
Central	155,827	157,588	158,829	2.91	2.91	2.44	0.79	0.71	0.63
Eastern	88,577	90,001	91,214	5.45	5.45	5.45	1.21	1.05	0.77
Northern	90,557	92,470	93,996	16.09	15.05	12.44	2.73	2.21	1.92
Western	102,916	104,369	105,585	5.50	3.70	3.70	0.65	0.51	0.45
Quintile									
Q1	23,786	24,734	25,655	n.a.	n.a.	n.a.	n.a.	n.a.	n.a.
Q2	35,267	36,164	37,344	n.a.	n.a.	n.a.	n.a.	n.a.	n.a.
Q3	48,720	49,755	50,814	n.a.	n.a.	n.a.	n.a.	n.a.	n.a.
Q4	71,820	73,062	74,702	n.a.	n.a.	n.a.	n.a.	n.a.	n.a.
Q5	187,730	189,844	190,999	n.a.	n.a.	n.a.	n.a.	n.a.	n.a.
Total	123,466	125,090	126,341	5.12	4.55	4.14	0.98	0.84	0.71

Source: Estimation using Uganda UNHS 2012/13 survey.
Note: n.a. = not applicable.

who do not have piped water but live in an area where other households have piped water, the baseline poverty incidence is 5.12 percent. This decreases by up to one percentage point with a connection (the decrease is a larger with the second than the first assumption). The counterfactual poverty gaps are also provided, and the proportional terms the gains in poverty reduction from connections to the network are similar (in absolute terms, the gains are smaller because the measures are low).

Conclusion

There are many potential benefits for households from a connection to the water network. This chapter focused on one of those benefits using the time use module of the last round of the Uganda National Household Survey for 2012/13 Piped water coverage may help household shift time from domestic to market work. These shifts are observed for women with a connection in the data, but not men. Simulations suggest that if piped water were provided to all households living in areas where the network is available at the neighborhood level, connections for households not yet connected would enable women to increase market work by about 1.5 hours on average. The poverty incidence in the sample would decrease by up to one percentage point, and the impact on the poverty gap would be similar in proportional terms. These gains may not seem large because the poverty measures are low, since the focus is on households living in areas with access—mostly Kampala and other large cities. But for those who may benefit from those gains, these gains in consumption can be very important.

Note

1. On various aspects of rural electrification in Uganda, see, for example, Ezor (2009), Hazal and Tedgren (2009), Muhoro (2010), Berg et al. (2011), and especially Government of the Republic of Uganda (2012).

References

Asian Development Bank. 2010. *Asian Development Bank's Assistance for Rural Electrification in Bhutan: Does Electrification Improve the Quality of Rural Life? Impact Evaluation Study*. Manila: Asian Development Bank.

Bardasi, E., and Q. Wodon. 2006. "Poverty Reduction from Full Employment: A Time Use Approach." In *Gender, Time Use and Poverty in Sub-Saharan Africa*, edited by C. M. Blackden and Q. Wodon. Washington, DC: World Bank.

———. 2008. "Who Pays the Most for Water? Alternative Providers and Service Costs in Niger." *Economics Bulletin* 9 (20): 1–10.

———. 2010. "Working Long Hours and Having No Choice: Time Poverty in Guinea." *Feminist Economist* 16 (3): 45–78.

Blackden, C. Mark, and Q. Wodon. 2006. *Gender, Time Use, and Poverty in Sub-Saharan Africa.* Washington, DC: World Bank.

Berg, C., M. Gaul, B. Korff, K. Raabe, J. Strittmatter, K. Tröger, and V. Tyumeneva. 2011. *Tracing the Impacts of Rural Electrification in West Nile, Uganda: A Framework and Toolbox for Monitoring and Evaluation.* Berlin: Humboldt-Universitat zu Berlin.

Dinkelman, T. 2008. *The Effects of Rural Electrification on Employment: New Evidence from South Africa.* Princeton, NJ: Princeton University.

Ezor, Z. 2009. *Power to the People: Rural Electrification in Uganda.* Uganda: School for International Studies.

Fay, M., D. Leipziger, Q. Wodon, and T. Yepes. 2007. "Achieving the Millennium Development Goals: The Role of Infrastructure." *World Development* 33 (8): 1267–84.

Government of the Republic of Uganda. 2012. *Rural Electrification Strategy and Plan Covering the Period 2013–2022.* Kampala: Ministry of Energy and Mineral Development.

Grogan, L., and A. Sadanand. 2008. "Electrification and the Household." Working Paper, University of Guelph.

Hazal, G., and C. Tedgren. 2009. "Establishing the Optimal Tariff in Rural Piped Water Distribution Networks A Case Study in Uganda." Master of Science Thesis, School of Electrical Engineering, KTH.

Ilahi, N. 2000. "The Intra-Household Allocation of Time and Tasks: What Have We Learnt from the Empirical Literature?" Policy Research Report on Gender and Development, Working Paper Series No. 13, World Bank, Washington, DC.

Ilahi, N., and F. Grimard. 2000. "Public Infrastructure and Private Costs: Water Supply and Time Allocation of Women in Rural Pakistan." *Economic Development and Cultural Change* 49: 45–75.

Khandker, S. R. 1996. "Education Achievements and School Efficiency in Rural Bangladesh." World Bank Discussion Paper No. 319, World Bank, Washington, DC.

Khandker, S. R., D. F. Barnes, and H. A. Samad. 2013. "Welfare Impacts of Rural Electrification: A Panel Data Analysis from Vietnam." *Economic Development and Cultural Change* 61: 659–92.

Martins, J. 2005. "The Impact Use of Energy Sources on the Quality of Life of Poor Communities." *Social Indicators Research* 72 (3): 373–402.

Muhoro, P. N. 2010. "Off-Network Piped Water Access and Its Impact on Micro-Enterprises: Evidence from Rural Uganda." PhD dissertation (Applied Physics), The University of Michigan, Ann Arbor.

Srivastava, L., and I. H. Rehman. 2006. "Energy for Sustainable Development in India: Linkages and Strategic Direction." *Energy Policy* 34 (5): 643–54.

Whittington, D., X. Mu, and R. Roche. 1990. "Calculating the Value of Time Spent Collecting Water: Some Estimates for Ukunda, Kenya." *World Development* 18 (2): 269–80.

World Bank. 2008. *The Welfare Impact of Rural Electrification: A Reassessment of the Costs and Benefits, Independent Evaluation Group.* Washington, DC: World Bank

PART 2

Tariffs, Subsidies, and Affordability

CHAPTER 5

Who Benefits from Subsidies for Piped Water?

Clarence Tsimpo and Quentin Wodon

Introduction

The extent to which households connected to the water network in Uganda benefit from subsidies is debatable. On the one hand, National Water and Sanitation Corporation (NWSC) is able to cover its operating costs and generate a profit margin. But on the other hand, many networks in small towns are not in the same position and thereby receive implicit or explicit subsidies from the government.

In many developing countries, it is tempting to subsidize residential piped water. Piped water is more and more considered as a basic necessity especially in urban areas. It is perceived to have important externalities for education and health. For many households in poverty, the full cost of a standard piped water bill may not be affordable. The desire to make piped water affordable to the poor and the population as a whole has led many governments and regulatory agencies to maintain piped water tariffs at low levels by not allowing tariffs to follow increases in production and distribution costs. Many governments also maintain increasing block tariff structures to ensure that the cost of piped water consumption is lower for households that consume smaller amounts of water. It is hoped that the implicit subsidies embedded in such tariff structures are targeted to the poor because households that consume lower amounts of water also tend to be poorer.

While the temptation is high to keep subsidizing piped water for residential customers through low average tariff levels and/or increasing block tariff structures, the cost of doing this may be high if the average level of the tariff is below cost-recovery levels for the utility (Estache et al. 2002; Foster and Briceno-Garmendia 2010; Ying et al. 2010; Estache and Wodon 2014; International Monetary Fund 2013). When subsidies are provided, they are often paid by the state, either directly or indirectly, and therefore compete with other priorities for public investments or social welfare programs. The subsidies may also distort price structures and incentives, and lead to inefficient use of piped water. The subsidies often reduce the ability of the utilities to carry adequate levels of maintenance for their networks and to invest more aggressively into production capacity and network extension. It is also not clear whether piped water consumption subsidies are well targeted to the poor, given that many among the poor lack access to the network. It could, for example, be that alternatives such as connection subsidies would be better for poverty reduction, or that changes in tariff structures could help in reducing overall subsidies while not hurting the poor too much, freeing resources for other policies more conducive to poverty reduction.

In Uganda, while subsidies for piped water are not as prominent as in many other countries, they seem to be present, at least to some extent and for some households. The National Water and Sewerage Corporation (NWSC) is able to cover its operating costs and generate a profit margin. But on the other hand, many networks in small towns are not in the same position and thereby receive implicit or explicit subsidies from the government. In small towns, the operational viability of water supply schemes is considered as attained by the Ministry of Water and Environment when revenues collected meet operating costs (and ideally generate some margin). For 55 out of 80 small towns, this was the case in 2012/13. But this does not factor in investment costs for expanding the network. For NWSC as well, the average unit cost of production is lower than the average tariff in many locations, and while, as just mentioned, the utility is able to cover operating costs as well as depreciation, with an operating profit used to fund investments, production costs have increased in recent years (in large part due to higher costs for energy used in water production). This made it necessary to apply a tariff increase in January 2012. Before that tariff increase, customers benefited implicitly from subsidies. Finally, the government and donors provide funding for network expansion which in a competitive market economy with fully private utilities might be funded from the utilities' revenues. One could thus suggest that at least to some extent, residential customers benefit from some level of subsidies for piped water in Uganda, in which case one could ask whether the subsidies are targeted to those most in need—the poor. Alternatively, if one is to argue that the sector is in fact broadly self-sufficient, at least in the case of NWSC, the question would then become who would benefit from new subsidies if these were to be provided to residential customers?

In order to answer this question, this chapter uses a simple framework to analyze the targeting performance to the poor of actual or potential subsidies. While most indicators of targeting performance are silent as of why subsidies are targeted the way they are (they only give an idea of whether the subsidies reach the poor or not and to what extent), the framework allows for analyzing access and subsidy design factors that affect targeting performance. Access factors are related to the availability of piped water service in the area where a household lives and to the household's choice to connect to the network when service is available. Subsidy factors relate to the tariff structure and the rate of subsidization of various types of customers. In Uganda, because of access factors, virtually none of actual or simulated consumption subsidies (would) benefit the poor. Connection subsidies could be better targeted. Section 2 describes the methodology. Section 3 provides the empirical results. As an alternative to poorly targeted consumption subsidies, section 4 looks at the potential targeting performance of connection subsidies. A brief conclusion follows.

Methodology for Consumption Subsidies

This section outlines the methodology used to assess who benefited from piped water subsidies (or potential subsidies, depending on one's interpretation of the financial sustainability requirement for the utilities) in Uganda until 2012. The methodology is reproduced from Angel-Urdinola and Wodon (2007; see also Angel-Urdinola, Cosgrove-Davies, and Wodon 2006, Komives et al. 2005, 2007; Banerjee et al. 2010; Angel-Urdinola and Wodon 2012 for applications to other countries).

Define by S_P and S_H the amounts of subsidies granted to the poor and to the population as a whole, respectively. The benefit targeting performance indicator Ω is the share of the subsidy benefits received by the poor (S_P/S_H) divided by the proportion of the population in poverty (P/H), where H denotes all households and P denotes the households that are poor. A value that is lower (greater) than one implies that the average subsidy for the poor is lower (greater) than the average subsidy received in the population as a whole. The parameter Ω can be computed from household surveys with data on expenditure on utility service, provided that information is also available on the tariff structure. The value of Ω is as follows:

$$\Omega = \frac{S_P}{S_H}\frac{H}{P} = \frac{\sum_{i=1}^{P} q_i(p_i - C)}{\sum_{i=1}^{H} q_i(p_i - C)}\frac{H}{P}$$

where q_i is the quantity consumed by household i and $p_i - C$ is the unit subsidy for household i (that is, the difference between average unit price for the household and unit cost of service C assumed constant across households.)

The parameter Ω can be decomposed in five key factors affecting its value: access, take-up, targeting, rate of subsidization, and quantity consumed. The first factor is access to the network in the neighborhood where the household lives, denoted by A, with typically access for the poor lower than for the population as a whole $(A_P < A_H)$. The second factor is take-up or usage of service when households have access, with often lower usage among the poor than the population as a whole conditional on access ($U_{P|A}<U_{H|A}$). The product of A and U is as before the connection or coverage rate (share of households using the service). The variables A and U affect the targeting performance of subsidies since in order to receive a subsidy households must first consume the good that is subsidized. The third factor is subsidy targeting (conditional on usage), which takes a value of one for households that receive a subsidy, and zero otherwise. When utility consumption is subsidized for all users, we have $T_{P|U}=T_{H|U}=1$. Beneficiary incidence (the probability of receiving or not the subsidy among a specific population group) is as follows:

$$B_H = A_H U_{H|A} T_{H|U}$$

$$B_P = A_P U_{P|A} T_{P|U}$$

To estimate the benefit incidence (as opposed to the beneficiary incidence), two more factors must be taken into account: the rate of subsidization and the quantity consumed among those who benefit from the subsidy. If the average quantity consumed by subsidy recipients in the population as a whole is $Q_{H|T}$, and the average expenditure on the good is $E_{H|T}$, the average rate of subsidization is $R_{H|T} = 1 - E_{H|T}/(Q_{H|T}\,C)$. The average value of the subsidy received among subsidy recipients is then $R_{H|T}\,Q_{H|T}\,C$. For the poor, the average subsidy received among those who benefit from the subsidy is $R_{P|T}\,Q_{P|T}\,C$. Overall, the average subsidy benefits in the population as a whole and among the poor are as follows:

$$\frac{S_H}{H} = B_H R_{H|T} Q_{H|T} C$$

$$\frac{S_P}{P} = B_P R_{P|T} Q_{P|T} C$$

This implies that:

$$\Omega = \frac{A_P}{A_H} \frac{U_{P|A}}{U_{H|A}} \frac{T_{P|U}}{T_{H|U}} \frac{R_{P|T}}{R_{H|T}} \frac{Q_{P|T}}{Q_{H|T}}$$

Thus, Ω is the product of five ratios for access, uptake, targeting, rate of subsidization, and quantity consumed. In most cases, the ratio of access rates will be lower than one (the poor tend to live in areas with lower access rates than the population as a whole), and the ratio of usage or take-up rates for the service will also be lower than one (when access is available in a neighborhood or village, the poor are less likely to be connected to the network than the population as a whole due to high costs of connection). Also, the quantities consumed in the population as a whole tend to be larger than those consumed by the poor. This means that the design of the subsidy mechanisms (through the values of T and R for the poor and the population as a whole) must be pro-poor if overall targeting is to be pro-poor (Ω larger than one).

In many countries, although not in Uganda, for piped water, water tariffs have an inverted block tariff structure (IBT). To better understand the design of such tariff structures and the implicit subsidy mechanisms they entail, denote as before by q_i the quantity consumed by a particular household i and by e_i the expenditure for that household. Consider first a benchmark case corresponding to an inverted block tariff structure with two price levels Π_A and Π_B with $\Pi_A < \Pi_B$. The reasoning can easily be extended to more blocks. The variable L denotes the consumption threshold (in cubic meters per month) at which the unit price for the good shifts from Π_A to Π_B. In IBTs, L is often considered as a "lifeline," that is a level of consumption needed for a household to meet its basic needs. If we denote by t_i a dummy variable taking a value of one for a household eligible to benefit from the lifeline rate (and a value of zero otherwise), the expenditure of household i is as follows:

$$[IBT] \quad e_i = \begin{cases} q_i\Pi_A & \text{if} \quad q_i \leq L \\ L\Pi_A + (q_i - L)\Pi_B & \text{if} \quad q_i > L \end{cases}, \text{ with } t_i = 1 \text{ if } \{q_i > 0\}.$$

In that equation, all households pay a unit price of Π_A per quantity consumed below the lifeline L, and for those who consume more than L, the price per unit consumed above that threshold is Π_B. Household with higher consumption will pay a higher average price per unit consumed, but since all households with a positive consumption benefit from the lower unit prices for quantities below L, the targeting indicator t_i is equal to one, meaning that every household consuming some quantity benefits from a lower unit price for at least part of the quantity consumed. An alternative tariff structure is to grant the lower price Π_A only to those households consuming less than L. This is referred to as a volume differentiated tariff (VDT):

$$[VDT] \quad e_i = \begin{cases} q_i\Pi_A & \text{if} \quad q_i \leq L \\ q_i\Pi_B & \text{if} \quad q_i > L \end{cases}, \text{ with } t_i = 1 \text{ if } \{q_i > 0 \text{ and } q_i \leq L\}.$$

In that equation, if total quantity consumed is above L, the unit price is Π_B, and this price applies to the total quantity consumed. In turn, since only the households who consume less than L benefit from the lower price Π_A, the targeting indicator takes a value of one only for those households. Under IBT and VDT tariff structures, these equations enable us to compute subsidy rates for the poor and the population as a whole under alternative tariff designs. If we denote the average subsidy rate for the poor R_P (among poor households that benefit for at least part of their consumption from a lower tariff rate as compared to the average cost for the utility), we have:

$$R_P = \left(1 - \frac{\sum_{i=1}^{P} e_i 1(p_i = 1)1(t_i = 1)}{C\sum_{i=1}^{P} q_i 1(p_i = 1)1(t_i = 1)}\right)$$

where p_i takes a value of one for a household in poverty and zero otherwise, and $1(p_i = 1)$ and $1(t_i = 1)$ are indicator functions taking a value of one if the conditions are met (that is, the household is poor in the first function, and the household benefits from a lower tariff rate on at least part of its consumption in the second function), and zero otherwise. Thus, only households verifying these conditions are included in the estimation of the ratio of expenditures to costs. The subsidy rate at the national level R_H is calculated likewise among all households that benefit from the subsidy:

$$R_H = \left(1 - \frac{\sum_{i=1}^{H} e_i 1(t_i = 1)}{C\sum_{i=1}^{H} q_i 1(t_i = 1)}\right)$$

Targeting Performance of Consumption Subsidies

In many developing countries, the piped water tariff follows an IBT structure, which means that the price per cubic meter increases with the quantity consumed by households. In Uganda, however, all customers pay the same flat rate per unit consumed, in addition to a fixed charge. In 2009/10, before the tariff increase of 2012, the unit price per cubic meter was U Sh 1,585. This increased to U Sh 1,912 per cubic meter in 2012/13 (see table 5.1). In 2005/06, the price was U Sh 879 per cubic meter. Given that the surveys provide data on the amounts paid by households for their piped water, it is feasible to estimate the level of consumption of households using these tariff structures. Figure 5.1 displays the density function for household piped water consumption in the 2009/10 and 2012/13 survey. The density functions for both survey years are fairly similar to each other, although consumption levels as measured in the survey are lower for 2012/13 than for 2009/10.

Table 5.1 Piped Water Tariff Structure at the Time of the Household Surveys

Year	Unit Price(U Sh per m³)
2005/06	879
2009/10	1585
2012/13	1912

Source: NWSC.
Note: For all years, the unit price was the same for all units. Service charge was not included.

Residential Piped Water in Uganda • http://dx.doi.org/10.1596/978-1-4648-0708-4

Figure 5.1 Density Function for Piped Water Consumption, 2009/10 and 2012/13

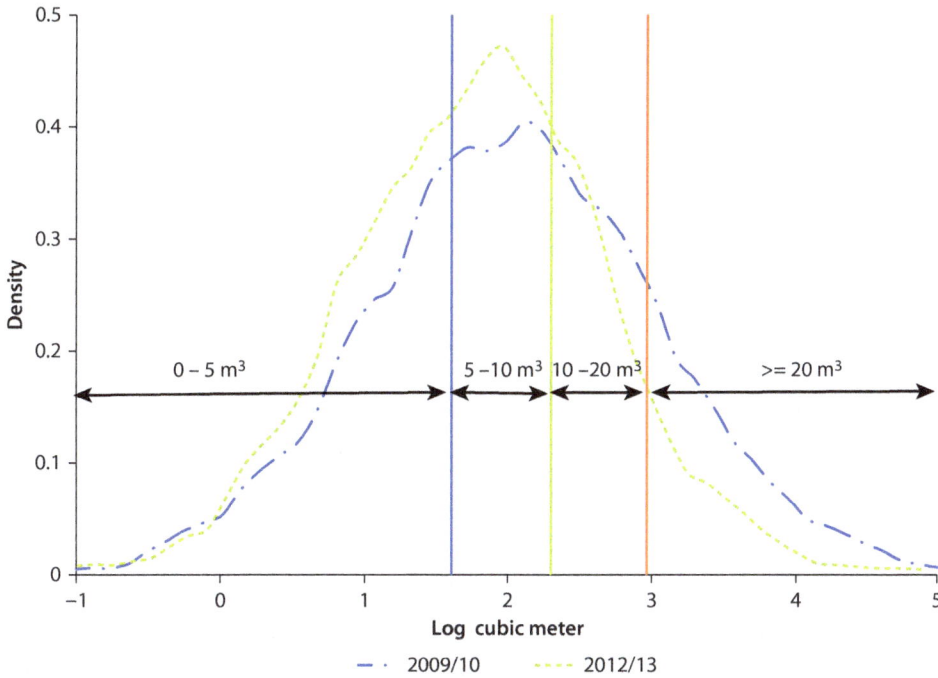

Source: Data from Uganda 2009/10 and 2012/13 UNHS surveys.

Table 5.2 provides data on piped water consumption for the three survey years at the national, urban, and rural levels by welfare decile. The statistics are provided only for households connected to the network. There is quite a bit of coherence in the data for the three years as the level of consumption in cubic meter does not change much over time. In 2012/13, at the national level, consumption per month among those connected to the network was on average at 8.5 cubic meter per month (6.1 cubic meter in rural areas versus 8.9 cubic meter in urban areas). Consumption levels were slightly higher in the two previous years at at 11.7 cubic meter on average nationally in 2009/10 and 11.8 cubic meter in 2005/06. As expected, consumption levels are higher among richer households. When taking into account connection rates (which are provided in chapter 2), it can be shown that the top decile typically accounts for most of the residential consumption, while the share accounted for by the bottom half of the population is well below 10 percent.

In order to estimate who benefits from the implicit subsidies in the tariff structure, we need to make an assumption regarding the cost of service. For simplicity, and in the absence of detailed data on the cost structure of the utilities, the "all inclusive" price per cubic meter (including, for example, provisions for network expansions) is assumed to be 20 percent higher than the flat rate charged by NWSC—this assumption does not actually affect the results.

Table 5.2 Piped Water Consumption among Those Connected, by Decile, 2005–13
Cubic meters

Decile	2005/06			2009/10			2012/13		
	National	Urban	Rural	National	Urban	Rural	National	Urban	Rural
1	2.5	7.7	3.0	14.2	3.6	14.2	0.5	14.1	0
2	6.4	5.4	4.5	0	3.5	0	14.1	6.2	0.5
3	7.4	8.7	6.5	4.6	7.2	5.5	6.2	7.0	0
4	11.5	5.2	10.2	3.4	5.0	0	4.3	6.2	0
5	7.0	6.3	11.6	5.1	9.9	3.5	7.1	7.2	1.6
6	9.6	10.7	5.1	8.3	6.4	9.1	7.5	10.6	10.5
7	6.4	11.8	11.1	6.4	9.2	8.2	7.1	8.2	5.6
8	8.3	17.1	7.3	8.0	8.5	9.4	9.3	7.5	9.8
9	11.0	20.6	7.8	7.9	17.3	9.2	7.5	8.9	5.6
10	14.2	13.6	6.8	15.0	13.8	15.1	10.0	12.1	5.0
All	11.7	14.0	7.3	11.8	11.3	13.0	8.5	8.9	6.1

Source: Data from Uganda 2005/06, 2009/10 and 2012/13 UNHS surveys.

The results from the decomposition analysis are provided in table 5.3. Note than in urban areas in 2009/10 and 2012/13, the decomposition does not work simply because there are no (or too few) households in poverty that live in urban areas and are connected to the network in those two years (in part because of the decline in poverty over time). In part for that reason, at the national level the value of Ω is essentially zero in 2012/13, although it is 0.03 in 2010/09 and 0.13 in 2005/06. Changes in targeting performance between the first and third years will be discussed below. But for all practical purposes, targeting performance is extremely low because virtually none among the poor are connected to the network due to lack of access and take-up when access is (at least in principle) available. In addition, because of the flat price for all customers (no lifeline bracket of consumption for customers consuming small amounts of water), the "subsidy design" factors do not play a meaningful role to improve targeting performance.

The official poverty measures for Uganda suggest that the share of households in poverty (P/H) was 26.5 percent in 2005/06, 19.3 percent in 2009/10, and 15.4 percent in 2012/13 (the share of the population in poverty is higher, at 31.1 percent in 2005/06, 24.5 percent in 2009/10, and 19.5 percent in 2012/13 because the poor tend to have larger household sizes on average). This results in share of the benefits reaching the poor (γ parameter with $\gamma = \Omega \times [P/H]$) of only 3 percent in 2005/06, 1/2 percent in 2009/10, and 0 percent in 2012/13.

One could argue that piped water subsidies are meant exclusively not only for the poor but also for other vulnerable households. What would happen if the definition of the target group were changed? Would the subsidies be better targeted? To a limited extent they would, but the gains would be small, because so many households connected to the network are concentrated in the top part of

Table 5.3 Targeting Performance of Piped Water Subsidies, 2005–13

	2005/06			2009/10			2012/13		
	National	Urban	Rural	National	Urban	Rural	National	Urban	Rural
	Detailed decomposition parameters								
A_N	0.1773	0.5523	0.0981	0.1798	—	0.0628	0.1980	—	0.0543
A_P	0.0865	0.3076	0.0711	0.0394	—	0.0222	0.0364	—	0.0114
$U_{N|A}$	0.1855	0.2234	0.1403	0.2448	—	0.2346	0.3439	—	0.2231
$U_{P|A}$	0.0913	0.0984	0.0891	0.0468	—	0.0881	0.0047	—	0.0168
$T_{N|U}$	1.0000	1.0000	1.0000	1.0000	—	1.0000	1.0000	—	1.0000
$T_{P|U}$	1.0000	1.0000	1.0000	1.0000	—	1.0000	1.0000	—	1.0000
$R_{N|T}$	0.2000	0.2000	0.2000	0.2075	—	0.2075	0.0440	—	0.0440
$R_{P|T}$	0.2000	0.2000	0.2000	0.2075	—	0.2075	0.0440	—	0.0440
$Q_{N|T}$	11.69	14.00	7.33	11.75	—	13.02	8.53	—	6.05
$Q_{P|T}$	6.57	6.64	6.54	7.65	—	7.65	0.52	—	0.52
	Ratios								
A	0.4880	0.5570	0.7243	0.2193	—	0.3539	0.1840	—	0.2102
U	0.4922	0.4404	0.6352	0.1912	—	0.3754	0.0136	—	0.0755
T	1.0000	1.0000	1.0000	1.0000	—	1.0000	1.0000	—	1.0000
R	1.0000	1.0000	1.0000	1.0000	—	1.0000	1.0000	—	1.0000
Q	0.5617	0.4747	0.8925	0.6507	—	0.5872	0.0613	—	0.0864
	Omega and gamma								
Ω	0.1349	0.1164	0.4106	0.0273	—	0.0780	0.0002	—	0.0014
γ	0.0357	0.0116	0.1232	0.0053	—	0.0175	0.0000	—	0.0003

Source: Data from the Uganda 2005/06, 2009/10, and 2012/13 UNHS surveys.

the distribution of consumption. Table 5.4 and figure 5.2 provide the values of Ω and γ for the 2012/13 survey under various definitions of the target group, considering "the poor" as representing the bottom 30 percent, 40 percent, 50 percent, 60 percent, and finally 70 percent of households (not population) in terms of consumption. Consider the share of the subsidies γ going to the various target groups so defined. Even when one considers the bottom 70 percent of households as the target group, γ takes on a value of only 10.6 percent, which is still very low.

What could be done to improve the targeting performance of piped water subsidies? Without poor households connected to the water network, the targeting performance of consumption subsidies will remain at zero. So the first step would be a network expansion targeting some among the poor. Once that is achieved, as explained in the methodological section, many countries have adopted IBT (or possibly VDT) tariff structures, whereby the unit price per cubic meter is lower for customers who consume a smaller amount of water. Experience suggests that reducing the levels of the so-called lifeline consump-

Table 5.4 Targeting Performance under Alternative Poverty Lines, 2012/13

	30% Poor	40% Poor	50% Poor	60% Poor	70% Poor
Targeting performance Ω	0.2790	0.3130	0.4130	0.5636	0.6578
Share benefitting the poor γ	0.0838	0.1253	0.2067	0.3383	0.4605

Source: Data from the Uganda 2009/10 UNHS surveys.

Figure 5.2 Omega and Gamma under Various Target Groups, 2012/13

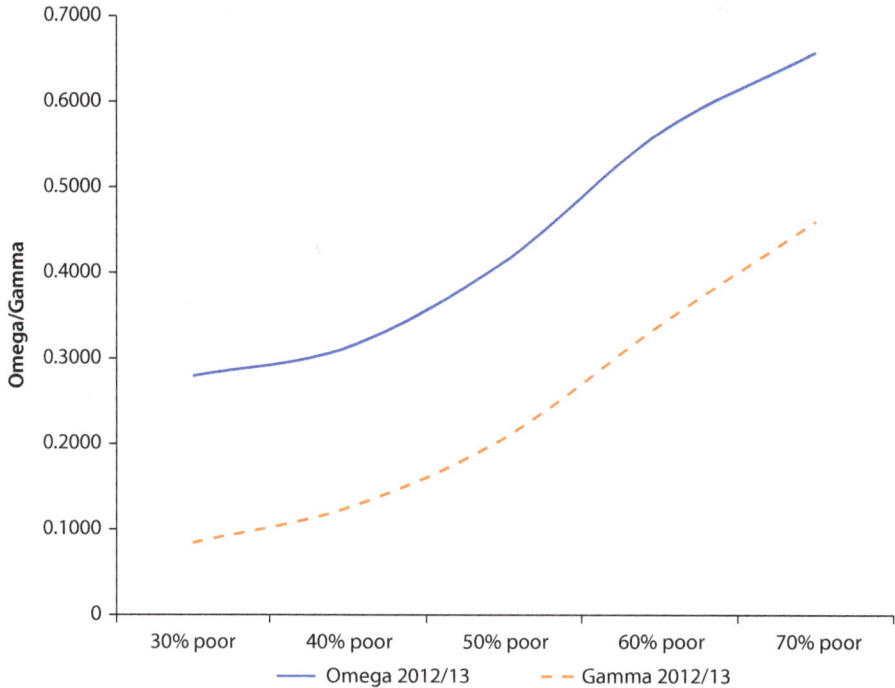

Source: Data from the Uganda 2012/13 UNHS survey.

tion level (the bottom bracket) in tariff structures may improve targeting performance, but only very slightly, while not necessarily reducing substantially the level of spending for subsidies (Komives et al. 2005). Another alternative explored in other countries to improve targeting performance is to implement VDTs instead of IBTs. As explained earlier, under VDTs only those customers consuming below a certain threshold are subsidized. Thus, instead of providing all customers with a subsidized first block of consumption as is the case in IBTs, VDTs provide a subsistence level of consumption at a lower price, but this lower price is accessible only to those who do not consume more than the subsistence level. VDTs typically improve targeting performance, but again only slightly, although they may also help reduce outlays for subsidies since only a subset of residential consumers are eligible to receive certain levels of subsidies.

In the case of Uganda, given the lack of access of the poor to the network, it is not clear that IBT or VDT tariff structures are worth implementing, and discussing their implications is beyond the scope of this chapter. But from the point of view of poverty reduction, the fact that piped water tariffs were increased in 2012 was warranted to avoid large and poorly targeted subsidies (implicit or explicit), since the impact of the increase on the poor will be negligible, given that so few among the poor are connected to the network (this is discussed in chapter 7).

Potential Targeting Performance of Connection Subsidies

Subsidies provided under tariff structures in Uganda do not (or would not) reach the poor because of a lack of access and take-up rates among them. An alternative could be to provide connection instead of consumption subsidies. There is indeed evidence from willingness to pay studies that many among the poor would like to connect to the network. Assuming that newly connected households would be on average poorer than households connected to the network, connection subsidies could lead to substantially higher values for Ω and γ.

To analyze the potential performance of connection subsidies, simple simulations can be implemented with the household surveys. Denote the average subsidy rate for a connection subsidy received by a household in the population benefitting from such subsidies by $R_{H|T}^C$. This rate depends on the difference between the average cost of a connection (C^C), assumed constant for all households for simplicity, and the connection fee actually paid by households (F_H^C). The rate of subsidization $R_{H|T}^C$ is then $R_{H|T}^C = 1 - F_{H|T}^C / C^C$. For the poor, it is $R_{P|T}^C = 1 - (F_{P|T}^C / C^C)$.

Three stylized scenarios for connections subsidies can be considered. First, we assume that connection subsidies are distributed in the same way as existing connections. This is a pessimistic assumption from a distributional point of view since it tends to favor better-off households, but it may be realistic when access rates are low. In that case:

$$\Omega^{C1} = \frac{A_P}{A_H} \frac{U_{P|A}}{U_{H|A}} \frac{R_{P|T}^C}{R_{H|T}^C}$$

Second, new connections could be distributed randomly among households that are not connected, but live in a neighborhood where access is available. In that case:

$$\Omega^{C2} = \frac{A_P}{A_H} \frac{(1 - U_{P|A})}{(1 - U_{H|A})} \frac{R_{P|T}^C}{R_{H|T}^C}$$

Residential Piped Water in Uganda • http://dx.doi.org/10.1596/978-1-4648-0708-4

Third, new connection subsidies could be randomly distributed among all households that do not currently have access (an optimistic assumption, given that many of these households do not live in neighborhoods with access). This would lead to:

$$\Omega^{C3} = \frac{(1 - A_P U_{P|A})}{(1 - A_H U_{H|A})} \frac{R^C_{P|T}}{R^C_{H|T}}$$

In most cases, one would observe that $\Omega^{C1} < \Omega^{C2} < \Omega^{C3}$, although this does not need mathematically to be the case. Table 5.5 provides the results, which are also visualized in figure 5.3. The simulations are again done with the 2012/13 survey. When connection subsidies are distributed to households similar to those with access, they are not well targeted. But under the other two scenarios, they are (of course) better targeted than consumption subsidies. In the second scenario, which assumes that households who benefit from new connections are selected from currently nonserved households living in areas with access, Ω is nationally at a value of 0.279. In the third scenario, which is the least realistic, targeting performance is above one.

While connection subsidies clearly have the potential to be better targeted than consumption subsidies, they should be implemented at scale only when generation capacity is sufficient, and when considered, they need to be implemented well to ensure good targeting and limit costs. This has not always been the case. In their study on social water connections in Abidjan and Dakar, Lauria and Hopkins (2004) explain how social connections were financed through a Water Development Fund paid for through a surcharge on water tariffs. Unfortunately, poor targeting resulted in 90 percent of residential connections in Abidjan being eligible for the subsidy. In fact, some of the connected households paying the surcharge were found to be poorer than many of the households receiving the new social connections. The program suffered from distorted incentives as flat fees paid for each social connection to private operators were an incentive for them to increase the number of subsidized connections while seeking for these "social" connection–richer households that were likely to consume more water (so that the utilities would reap higher revenues) and were located closer to the pipes (to minimize the cost of connecting). According to the authors, these distortions may in fact have led to reductions in connection rates (or at least delays in the time needed for connection) among poor households that lived in informal settlements. The fact that the social connections required households to own the land on which their dwelling was located also probably undermined the targeting performance of the program. This example makes it clear that for connection as well as for consumption subsidies, good design of the subsidy mechanism is required for the subsidy to actually reach the poor.

Table 5.5 Simulated Targeting Performance of Connection Subsidies, 2009/10

	National	Urban	Rural
Case 1: New connections mirror the distribution of existing connections	0.003	0.000	0.016
Case 2: New connections for households with access but no connection	0.279	0.621	0.266
Case 3: New connections to randomly selected households not connected	1.073	1.285	1.012

Source: Data from Uganda 2005/06 and 2009/10 UNHS survey.

Figure 5.3 Simulated Targeting Performance of Connection Subsidies, 2012/13

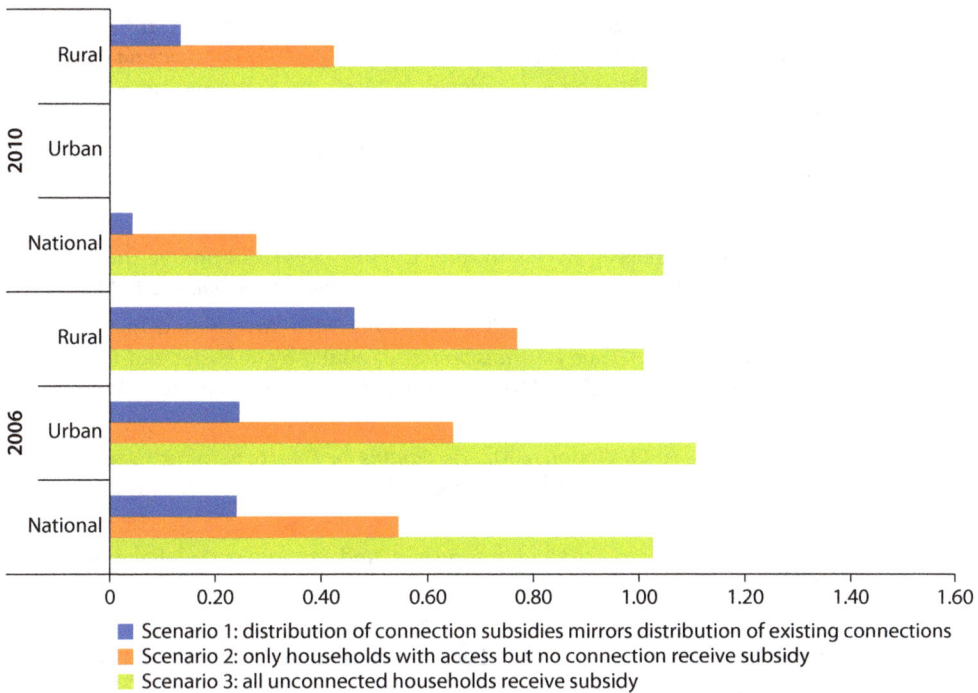

■ Scenario 1: distribution of connection subsidies mirrors distribution of existing connections
■ Scenario 2: only households with access but no connection receive subsidy
■ Scenario 3: all unconnected households receive subsidy

Source: Data from the Uganda 2012/13 UNHS survey.

Conclusion

This chapter was devoted to an assessment of the targeting performance to the poor of (actual or potential) subsidies embedded in the tariff structure for piped water. The framework for this assessment allowed for measuring both "access" and "subsidy design" factors that affect targeting performance. Due to very low connection rates to piped water among the poor, piped water subsidies are (or would be) very poorly targeted. In 2012/13, none of the subsidies reached the poor. Changing some of the parameters of the tariff structure, such as introducing blocks through an IBT or VDT tariff structure would not improve the targeting performance simply because of the weight of access factors. By contrast, providing connection subsidies as opposed to consumption subsidies might

Residential Piped Water in Uganda • http://dx.doi.org/10.1596/978-1-4648-0708-4

increase the share of the subsidies that would be received by the poor. Overall, these results are not surprising, but they provide a useful quantification of basic parameters that can inform policy toward access and affordability of piped water in Uganda. From the point of view of poverty reduction, increasing piped water tariffs in 2012 was the right thing to do, simply because virtually none of the poor are connected to the network according to the latest household survey, so that subsidies do not reach the poor.

References

Angel-Urdinola, D., M. Cosgrove-Davies, and Q. Wodon. 2006. "Rwanda: Piped Water Tariff Reform." In *Poverty and Social Impact Analysis of Reforms Lessons and Examples from Implementation*, edited by A. Coudouel, A. Dani, and S. Paternostro. Washington, DC: World Bank.

Angel-Urdinola, D., and Q. Wodon. 2007. "Do Utility Subsidies Reach the Poor? Framework and Evidence for Cape Verde, Sao Tome, and Rwanda." *Economics Bulletin* 9 (4): 1–7.

———. 2012. "Does Increasing Access to Infrastructure Services Improve the Targeting Performance of Water Subsidies?" *Journal of International Development* 24 (1): 88–101.

Banerjee, S., Q. Wodon, and V. Foster. 2010. "Dealing with Poverty and Inequality." In *Africa's Infrastructure: A Time for Transformation*, edited by V. Foster and C. Briceno-Garmendia. Washington, DC: Africa Development Forum, Agence Française de Développement and World Bank.

Estache, A., V. Foster, and Q. Wodon. 2002. *Accounting for Poverty in Infrastructure Reform: Learning from Latin America's Experience*. Washington, DC: World Bank, WBI Development Studies.

Estache, A., and Q. Wodon. 2014. *Infrastructure and Poverty in Sub-Saharan Africa*. New York: Palgrave Macmillan.

Foster, V., and C. Briceno-Garmendia, eds. 2010. *Africa's Infrastructure: A Time for Transformation*. Africa Development Forum. Washington, DC: Agence Française de Développement and World Bank.

International Monetary Fund. 2013. *Case Studies on Energy Subsidy Reform: Lessons and Implications*. Washington, DC: International Monetary Fund.

Komives, K., V. Foster, J. Halpern, and Q. Wodon. 2005. *Water, Piped Water, and the Poor: Who Benefits from Utility Subsidies?* Washington, DC: World Bank, Directions in Development.

Komives, K., J. Halpern, V. Foster, Q. Wodon, and R. Abdullah. 2007. "Utility Subsidies as Social Transfers: An Empirical Evaluation of Targeting Performance." *Development Policy Review* 25 (6): 659–79.

Lauria, D., and O. Hopkins. 2004. *Pro-Poor Subsidies for Water Connections: Cases from West Africa*. Chapel Hill: University of North Carolina.

Ying, Y., H. Skilling, S. Banerjee, Q. Wodon, and V. Foster. 2010. "Cost Recovery, Equity, and Efficiency in Water Tariffs: Evidence from African Utilities." Policy Research Working Paper No. 5384, World Bank, Washington, DC.

CHAPTER 6

Targeting Performance of Piped water Subsidies in Africa

Clarence Tsimpo and Quentin Wodon

Introduction

As shown in the previous chapter, piped water subsidies in Uganda are (or would be) very poorly targeted. How does Uganda compare to other Sub-Saharan countries? Using the same framework as in chapter 5, this chapter compares the targeting performance of piped water subsidies in 19 countries, including Uganda. The influence of access factors on targeting performance is such that the subsidies in the various countries tend to be poorly targeted in general. However, in no other country are they as poorly targeted as in Uganda. The chapter also considers the potential performance of connection subsidies under various scenarios—these subsidies would in all likelihood be better targeted to the poor than existing consumption subsidies.

In Uganda, piped water subsidies are (or would be) very badly targeted to the poor. It may be interesting to compare the targeting performance of the subsidies in Uganda with the performance of subsidies embedded in the tariff structures of other Sub-Saharan African countries. This is the purpose of this chapter, which also considers connection subsidies.

Even though subsidies for piped water are often poor policy in the African context (Estache et al. 2002; Komives et al. 2005; Banerjee, Wodon, and Foster 2010; International Monetary Fund 2013; Alleyne 2013; Estache and Wodon 2014), the reasons why many countries subsidize piped water are not hard to understand. Governments aim to make piped water affordable for the population, including the poor. When increases in energy and other prices lead to higher utility costs, many utilities do not reflect these higher costs fully in their piped water tariff structures. As a result, many utilities are not able to cover their costs, or if they do, they often cannot afford to properly maintain their network, let alone expand it (the lack of proper maintenance of, and investments in, existing networks may in fact be an implicit subsidy in itself since customers then do not pay for costs that will have to be paid by others—typically the government, at some point). Increasing tariffs is also politically difficult for governments since such increases are highly visible for customers who will feel it right away, while they may not know much about the medium-term cost structures of the utilities and the need for increases. Such increases in tariffs affect urban populations the most, but these are precisely the populations that are most likely to be vocal, maybe even take up to streets against such increases.

While the temptation is high to keep subsidizing piped water tariffs for residential customers (as well as in some cases for commercial and industrial customers), the cost of doing this is however potentially high. The cost of producing and distributing piped water is often high in at least some African countries, in part because the populations served by the piped water tend to be small, which prevents to some extent the utilities to reap the full benefit of economies of scale. In addition, many countries are landlocked, with high transportation costs, and limited hydroelectric power, which also contributes to high generation costs due to the need to rely on thermal power including for the production of water (for example, for pumping). Thus, due to increasing production costs, subsidies that may appear to be limited at the household level tend to be expensive at the macroeconomic level, especially when compared to the limited resources available to governments through taxation and aid. Said differently, under strict budget constraints, subsidizing piped water has a direct cost in terms of crowding out today or in the future (typically through the accumulation of debt for the utilities that are often guaranteed by governments) resources for public interventions aimed at poverty reduction and development.

In addition, there is an additional perverse incentive that derives from the inability of utilities to cover their costs due to low tariffs. When utilities are operating at a loss, or at least cannot properly fund their maintenance and investment needs, they have no incentives to expand the network, since expanding the network would probably imply increasing their losses. At the margin, new customers may be poorer than existing customers, thereby increasing the cost of delivery and also increasing the risk of nonpayment. Furthermore, when investments are not sufficient, expanding the network to new customers is also problematic because of the limited production capacity, which may already translate into service cuts during the day. Finally, adding consumption through an expansion of the network often tends to further increase the average cost of producing water, since at the margin, even when countries have access to cheap production inputs, the additional demand may have to be met at a higher production costs.

The upshot of the above is that many utilities are trapped in a vicious circle. It can be shown that for the poor, the benefits of network extension are substantially larger than the benefits from the subsidization of water consumption. At the same time, without enough revenues to cover their operating and maintenance costs fully, utilities cannot seriously think about network expansions, as this might exacerbate their losses. In addition, poor quality of service, which is in part the consequence of the lack of revenues, limits the willingness of customers to pay a higher price for a service that is considered by them as deficient, due, for example, to service cuts during the day. As to regulatory agencies and governments, when hit by substantial price increases for inputs, and thereby for the cost of producing water, they are under pressure to reduce existing subsidies, especially in the context of their broader commitment to implement poverty reduction and development strategies. But the fear of discontent in the population makes such a reduction in subsidies difficult to implement. All parties are trapped in a situation that does not benefit them, with limited ability to move forward.

In this context, the contribution of this chapter is to try to demonstrate a simple fact: that piped water subsidies are among the least well-targeted subsidies that governments can implement, and that therefore the argument regarding the need to preserve these subsidies in order to make the service affordable for the poor, while valid for the small fraction of the poor who may already be connected to the network, does not hold when considering what is required to accelerate poverty reduction and economic development more broadly, including through network expansion. Said differently, even if some poor households would be hurt by a removal or substantial reduction in piped water subsidies that are prevailing in many countries, the gains that could be achieved by reallocating the resources now allocated to these subsidies could be very large, with many other poor households benefiting, and with a restoration of sustainability and profitability in the sector also conducive to growth itself.

The structure of the chapter is as follows. Section 2 introduced the methodology used for the analysis, as well as the data sources. In section 3, the data are used to estimate the targeting performance of consumption subsidies embedded in the residential tariff structures for piped water. The framework for the analysis is the same as that used in chapter 5, and it demonstrates clearly not only that piped water subsides are poorly targeted but also why in terms of access and subsidy design factors. Section 4 discusses, again as done in chapter 5 for Uganda, the potential targeting performance of connection subsidies. A brief conclusion follows.

Methodology and Data

This chapter applies the subsidy decomposition framework presented in chapter 5 to household survey data from 19 African countries (on this methodology, see Angel-Urdinola and Wodon [2007, 2012]). In terms of methodology, as a brief reminder (this was already discussed in chapter 5), define by S_P and S_H the amounts of subsidies granted to the poor and to the population as a whole, respectively. The benefit targeting performance indicator Ω is the share of the subsidy benefits received by the poor (S_P/S_H) divided by the proportion of the population in poverty (P/H), where H denotes all households and P denotes the households that are poor. A value that is lower (greater) than one implies that the average subsidy for the poor is lower (greater) than the average subsidy received in the population as a whole. The targeting parameter Ω can be decomposed in five key factors affecting its value: access, take-up, targeting, rate of subsidization, and quantity consumed.

The first factor is access to the network in the neighborhood where the household lives, denoted by A, with access for the poor often lower than for the population as a whole (typically $A_P < A_H$). The second factor is take-up or usage of service when households have access, with often lower usage among the poor than the population as a whole conditional on access (typically, $U_{P|A} < U_{H|A}$). The product of A and U is as before the connection or coverage rate (share of households using piped water from the network). The variables A and U affect the targeting performance of subsidies since in order to receive a subsidy households must first consume the good that is subsidized. The third factor is subsidy targeting (conditional on usage), which takes a value of one for households that receive a subsidy, and zero otherwise. When utility consumption is subsidized for all users as is the case with a traditional inverted block tariff (IBT) structure, we have $T_{P|U} = T_{H|U} = 1$. The last two factors are the rate of subsidization of piped water among those benefiting from subsidies versus the cost of providing the service (typically, $R_{P|T} > R_{H|T}$) and the quantity consumed among those who benefit from the subsidy (typically, $Q_{P|T} < Q_{H|T}$). The value of the targeting parameter Ω can be shown to be equal to:

$$\Omega = \frac{A_P}{A_H} \frac{U_{P|A}}{U_{H|A}} \frac{T_{P|U}}{T_{H|U}} \frac{R_{P|T}}{R_{H|T}} \frac{Q_{P|T}}{Q_{H|T}}$$

As already mentioned, in most cases, the ratio of access rates will be lower than one (the poor tend to live in areas with lower access rates than the population as a whole), and the ratio of usage or take-up rates for the service will also be lower than one (when access is available in a neighborhood or village, the poor are less likely to be connected to the network than the population as a whole due to high costs of connection). The quantities consumed in the population as a whole tend to be larger than those consumed by the poor. This means that the design of the subsidy mechanisms (through the values of T and R for the poor and the population as a whole) must be highly pro-poor if overall targeting is to be pro-poor (Ω larger than one), and this is very rarely (if not ever) the case with existing tariffs in Sub-Saharan African countries.

As was the case in chapter 5, we also simulate connection subsidies as an alternative to consumption subsidies. Three stylized scenarios are considered. First, we assume that connection subsidies are distributed in the same way as existing connections, leading to a first estimate of potential targeting performance Ω^{CI}. This is a pessimistic assumption from a distributional point of view since it tends to favor better-off households, but it may be realistic when access rates are low. Second, we assume that new connections are distributed randomly among households who are not connected, but live in a neighborhood where access is available (Ω^{C2} estimate). Third, we assume that new connection subsidies are randomly distributed among all households that do not currently have access (Ω^{C3} estimate, which is optimistic assumption, given that many of these households do not live in neighborhoods with access). In most cases, we would expect that $\Omega^{C1} < \Omega^{C2} < \Omega^{C3}$, although this does not need to be the case. If we assume that the connection costs and connection subsidies are the same for all households, the three estimates are defined as follows:

$$\Omega^{C1} = \frac{A_P}{A_H} \frac{U_{P|A}}{U_{H|A}} \qquad \Omega^{C2} = \frac{A_P}{A_H} \frac{(1-U_{P|A})}{(1-U_{H|A})} \qquad \Omega^{C3} = \frac{(1-A_P \times U_{P|A})}{(1-A_H \times U_{H|A})}$$

In terms of data, we rely on household surveys, which for most countries are from the middle of the last decade, because this work was initially done in 2008 for a report on infrastructure needs in Africa. In the case of Uganda, however, we use the results from the 2012/13 survey presented in the previous chapter. While for the other countries more recent surveys are often available, as was shown in the analysis for Uganda for the period 2005 to 2013 in chapter 5, the value of the targeting parameter Ω does not actually change very much in absolute percentage point terms from one year to the next because access and take-up rates do not change too much either, and the structure of tariff structures does not tend to be altered much either from one year to the next. This implies that at least for illustrative and comparative purposes of the targeting of Uganda's subsidies (actual or potential) with the subsidies in other Sub-Saharan African countries, the results essentially remain valid.

The surveys provide information on how much households spend on piped water. The tariff structures prevailing at the time of the survey are used to obtain the level of consumption of the household in terms of cubic meter per month. For standardization, in the absence of detailed data on the cost structure of the utilities, the price per cubic meter of the highest bracket in the tariff structure for residential customers is typically assumed to represent cost. The estimation of the targeting performance of the subsidies is however not very sensitive to the choice of the parameter to represent costs. Given that in most cases, the average price paid by customers is well below the cost of provision, the use of the highest bracket as an approximation for costs seems reasonable.

The list of countries included in the estimation and the corresponding household survey year for each country is as follows: Burkina Faso (2003); Burundi (2006); Cameroon (2001); Cape Verde (2006); Central African Republic (2007); Chad (2003); Democratic Republic of Congo (2005); Côte d'Ivoire (2001); Gabon (2005); Ghana (2006); Guinea (2003); Malawi (with two utilities, survey for 2004), Niger (2005); Nigeria (with two utilities, survey for 2005); Republic of Congo (2005); Rwanda (2001); Senegal (2001); Togo (2005); and Uganda (2009/10). The tariff structures in most countries were traditional IBT structures (see Ying et al. 2010, for a discussion of tariff structures in African countries).

Consumption Subsidies

In order to facilitate the visualization of the results, we rely in this chapter on graphical representations of the estimates instead of tables. Figure 6.1 gives the values of Ω for the consumption subsidies embedded in the tariff structures of the 19 countries. In all cases, the value of Ω is much lower than one, suggesting that on average the benefits from the subsidies going to the poor are much lower than for the population as a whole. Senegal, the Central African Republic (in part because of a very high poverty rate), and Gabon are the countries with the highest values of Ω, followed by the Democratic Republic of Congo and one of the two utilities in Nigeria. For the other countries, the values are below 0.50 so that on average the subsidy received by a poor household is less than half that received by a randomly selected household in the overall population. The values of Ω in some countries are extremely low (in Uganda, as already discussed in chapter 5, but also in especially in Burkina Faso, Burundi, Ghana, Guinea, Malawi, and Rwanda). In eight countries, the values are between about a fourth and half (Cameroon, Cape Verde, Chad, Côte d'Ivoire, Niger, Nigeria FCT, the Democratic Republic of Congo [La République démocratique du Congo (RDC) in French], and Togo).

Access rates as well as take-up rates when access is available are key factors that contribute to weak targeting performance for existing subsidies. First, access is often not available, especially in the areas where the poor live $(A_P < A_H)$. Furthermore, poor households having at least in principle access

Figure 6.1 Targeting Performance of Piped Water Subsidies, Selected Countries

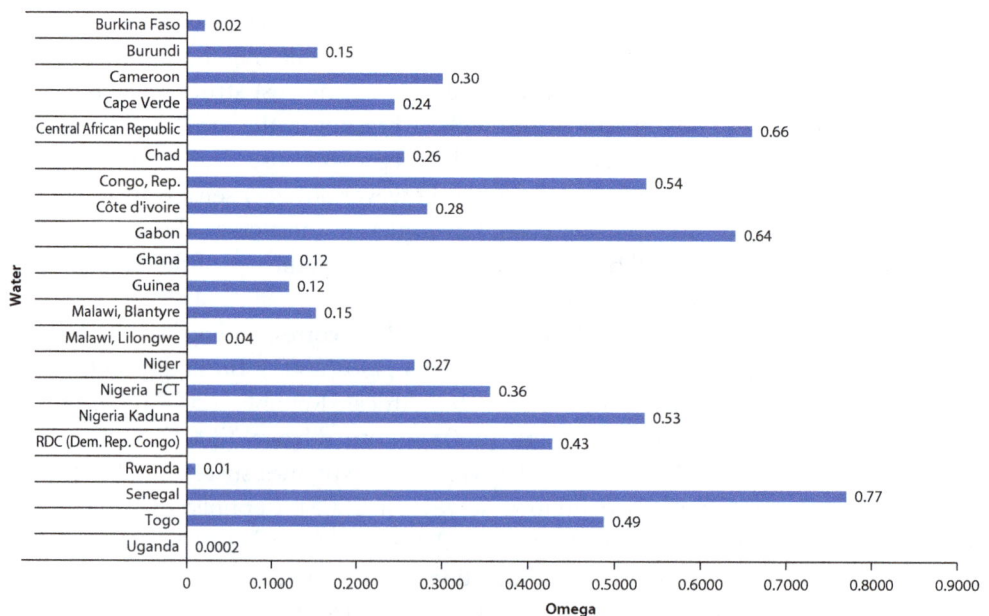

Source: Calculations using country-specific household surveys.

to the network in there are also less likely than the average household living in an area with access to use the service, whether this is because they may not be able to afford to pay for piped water, or because even if access is available in the area, the network may still be located too far away from their dwelling. In terms of the methodological framework, this means that $U_{Hl}A <$ $U_{Pl}A$. The combination of the values obtained for A and $U|A$ gives the actual connection or coverage rates in the population as a whole and among the poor. Figure 6.2 displays the values of A and $U|A$ for the population as a whole and for the poor.

Beyond differences in access and take-up rates between the poor and the overall population, poor subsidy design also limits the targeting performance of consumption subsidies. The subsidies are meant to benefit the poor. This is supposed to be the case for IBT tariffs, assuming that the poor have much lower levels of consumption than the population as a whole. But since IBTs enable all residential customers to benefit from subsidies in the lower brackets of consumption, they also benefit households that are better off, unless the upper tariffs in the IBT schedule are such that the subsidy provided to the better off in lower consumption brackets is reduced by a surcharge for the consumption in the higher brackets, but this is rarely the case in Sub-Saharan Africa because tariffs rarely achieve full cost recovery. Thus, under an IBT structure, all households typically benefit from at least some level of subsidy, and the targeting parameter $T|U$ is equal to one for both the population as a whole and the poor.

What about the rates of subsidization and the quantities consumed, namely the parameters $R|T$ and $Q|T$ in the framework? Figure 6.3 displays the product of these two parameters in the 19 countries. In many countries, the parameter $R|T$ is higher for the poor than the population as a whole (noting that this parameter is estimated under strong assumptions), but this is more than compensated for parameters $Q|T$, which is substantially higher for the population as a whole than the poor. Taking account of the assumed rate of subsidization, the quantity consumed by the beneficiaries of the subsidy determines the total value of the subsidy received. Figure 6.3 displays the product of the last two ratios in the estimation of Ω. The figure suggests that although rates of subsidization are higher for the poor than the overall population (because the poor consume less on average, hence pay tariffs associated with lower blocks of the IBT schedules), the differences are not large enough to compensate for the higher consumption levels among the overall population than the poor. In most countries, the product of the three subsidy design factors takes a value below one, contributing to poor targeting. Uganda is an outlier due to the fact that with a flat tariff structure, the ratio of quantities drives the results.

Figure 6.4 summarizes the evidence provided in the previous Figures by providing a scatter plot of the access and subsidy design factors affecting targeting performance, so that Ω = (access factors) x (subsidy design factors). The two access factors are whether a household lives in an area served by the network,

Figure 6.2 Access to and Usage of Piped Water Services, Selected Countries

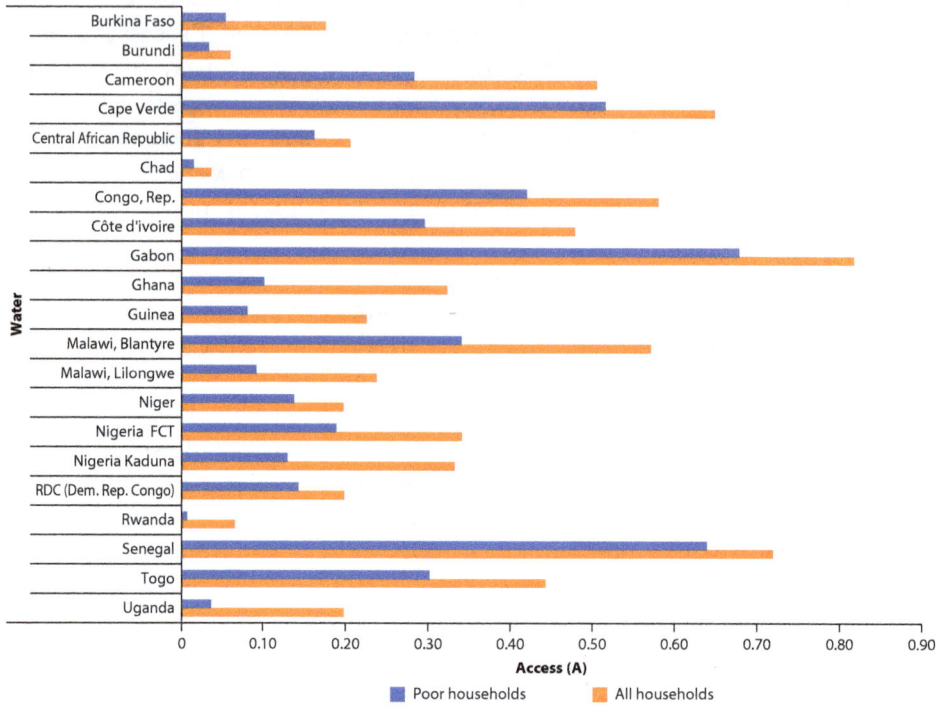

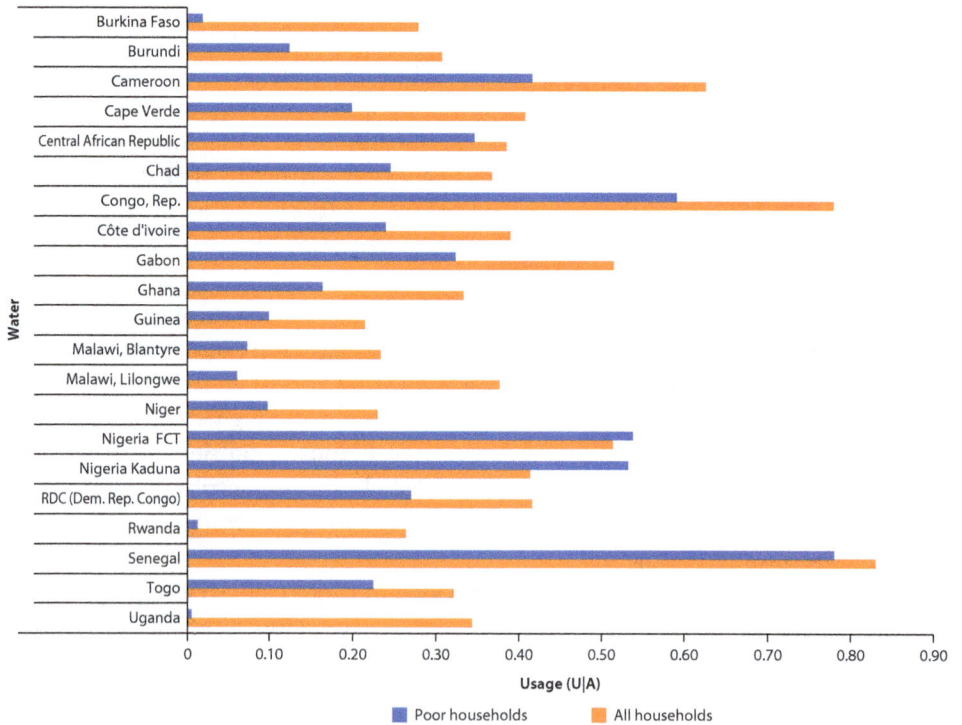

Figure 6.3 Product of the Subsidy Design Factors, Selected Countries

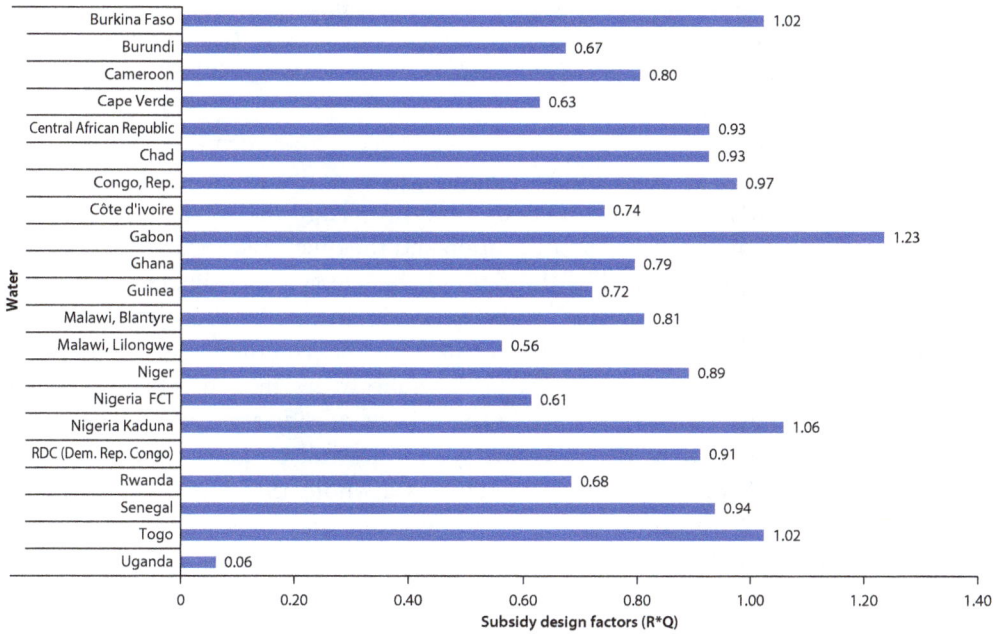

Source: Calculations using country-specific household surveys.

Figure 6.4 Access and Subsidy Design Factors Affecting Targeting Performance

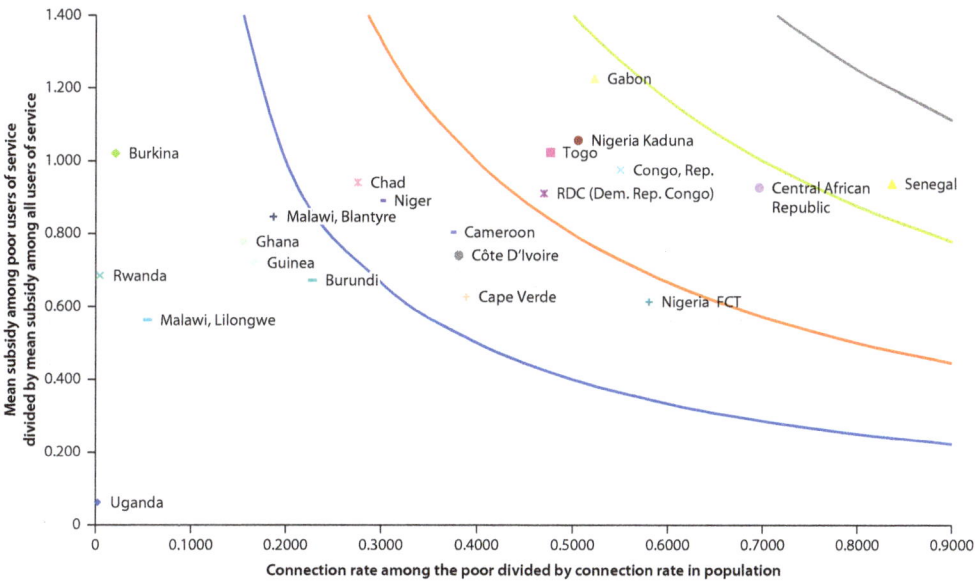

and when this is the case, whether the household is actually connected to the gird (that is, whether the household actually "takes up" the service). The value of the access factors variable is thus the rate of connection or coverage among the poor to the network (which depends on access and uptake when there is access) divided by the rate of connection in the population as a whole. This variable is presented on the horizontal axis in figure 6.4, and as expected, it is much lower than one for all countries simply because the poor have much lower connection rates than the population as a whole on average.

The second aggregate variable affecting targeting performance is related to subsidy design and takes into account who benefits from subsidies among households connected to the network and how large the subsidies are, which itself depends on the rate of subsidization and the quantity consumed. What the vertical axis represents is thus the ratio of the average subsidy among all poor households that are connected to the network, divided by the average subsidy among all households connected to the network, whether poor or nonpoor. Again, in all countries, the products of the subsidy design factors take on values below one. The reason is that while the rate of subsidization of the poor who are connected (that is, the discount versus the full cost of service) is often larger than for the population connected as a whole, the quantities consumed by all the poor who connected tend to be lower than those consumed by the overall connected population. Therefore, the average subsidy received by the poor who are connected is lower than for the overall connected population (note that in all countries, we have T/U equal to one for the poor and the overall population connected).

The countries placed lowest on the scatter plot in figure 6.4 (the bottom left corner) have the worst targeting performance, and this includes Uganda, as discussed earlier. The curves through the scatter plot indicate equal values for the targeting performance parameter Ω.

What could be done to improve targeting performance? As discussed in chapter 5, the experience suggests that reducing the levels of consumption for the first bracket of the tariff structure (the "lifeline") in countries with an IBT structure does not lead to a large gain in targeting performance. One alternative is to implement instead volume differentiated tariffs (VDTs). Under VDTs, only those customers consuming below a certain threshold are subsidized. Thus, instead of providing all customers with a subsidized first block of consumption as is the case in IBTs, VDTs provide a subsistence level of consumption at a lower price, but this lower price is accessible only to those who do not consume more than the subsistence level. VDTs typically do improve targeting performance, although in most cases not by much, but their main benefit is that they may help in reducing the overall cost of subsidies. Another alternative is connection subsides, which are discussed next.

Connection Subsidies

Changing subsidy design factors has the potential to improve targeting performance, but probably not to satisfactory levels. This is because the subsidies provided under the tariff structures do not solve the underlying issue of a lack of access and take-up rates among the poor. Using geographic targeting or proxy means testing may also bring better results in terms of targeting performance, but these targeting systems are not practical to implement in many Sub-Saharan African countries. One other alternative to improve targeting performance could be to provide connection instead of consumption subsidies. Assuming that newly connected households are poorer than households already benefiting from connections, this could lead to higher values for Ω. Figure 6.5 provides estimates of potential targeting performance for connection subsidies under the three scenarios considered in the methodological discussion in section 2. As expected, the value of Ω is largest under the assumption that new connections benefit households that are selected randomly from the population without a connection. In all cases, Omega is larger than one under that assumption. Yet, the assumption is not realistic, because many of those households are located in areas that are not yet served by the network. The second scenario assumes that households that benefit from new connections are selected from currently nonconnected households living in areas where there is already access to the network. The values of Omega in that case, while often lower than one, are still much better than the targeting performance of existing consumption subsidies. In the third scenario, new connections are distributed in a similar way to existing connections, in which case targeting remains poor.

Figure 6.5 Potential Targeting Performance of Connection Subsidies

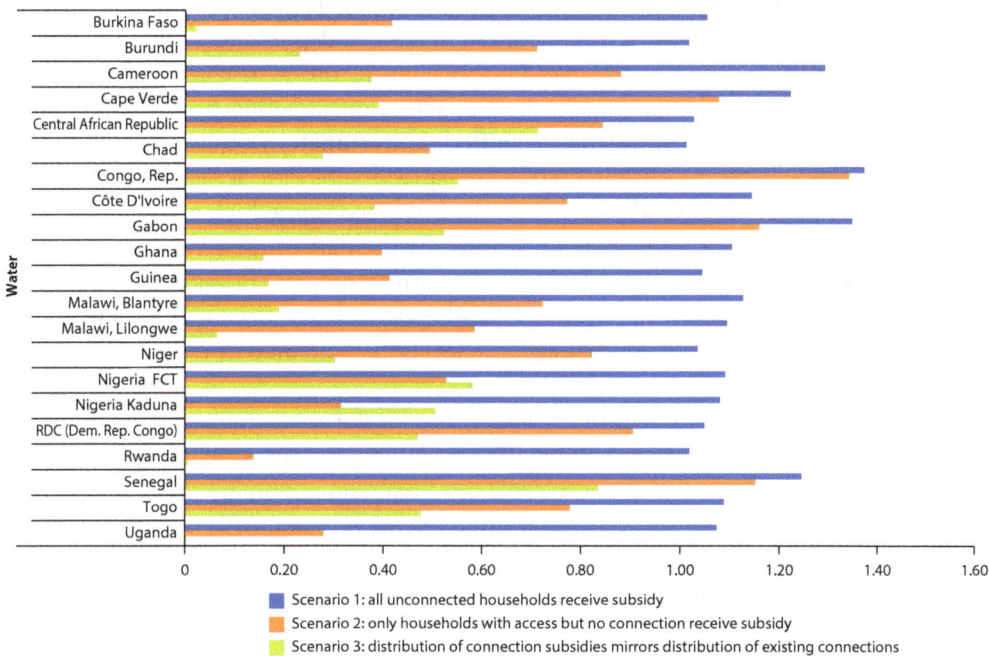

Scenario 1: all unconnected households receive subsidy
Scenario 2: only households with access but no connection receive subsidy
Scenario 3: distribution of connection subsidies mirrors distribution of existing connections

Note: FCT = Federal Capital Territory.

As was the case in chapter 5, it should be noted however that while connection subsidies have potential, they need to be implemented well to ensure good targeting and limit costs. In their study on social water connections in Abidjan and Dakar, Lauria and Hopkins (2004) show that connection subsidies for piped water in Côte d'Ivoire were not well targeted. The program suffered from distorted incentives as flat fees paid for each "social" connection to private operators led them to maximize subsidized connections especially among households that did not need them (targeting better-off households helped the utilities reap higher revenues with lower connection costs as those households tend to be located closer to the network). These distortions may have led to a reduction in connections for the poor living in informal settlements. This example makes it clear that for connection subsidies as well, proper design is important.

Conclusion

Several clear messages emerge from the analysis of the targeting performance of piped water subsidies and the decomposition of this targeting performance into key factors driving it. Overall, consumption subsidies for piped water appear to be very poorly targeted in African countries, including Uganda. Several reasons explain this poor performance. First, access factors are important in determining the potential beneficiaries of consumption subsidies. When poor households live in areas without service, it is impossible for them to connect to the network. Even when there is potential access to the service where the poor live, many among the poor remain not connected, either because they live still too far from the network or because the cost of connecting and purchasing the equipment needed to use piped water may be too high. In order to compensate for the negative impact of access and take-up factors on targeting performance, good subsidy design mechanisms are required. Unfortunately, traditional IBT structures tend to be poorly targeted. They spread subsidies across all households connected to the network, since even those who consume high amounts of piped water benefit from some level of subsidy for the part of their consumption that belongs to the lower-level blocks of the tariff structure. In addition, the lower blocks in many countries (not in Uganda which has a flat tariff structure) are often too high in terms of consumption levels in cubic meter per month to target the poor well.

One alternative to improve the targeting performance of piped water subsidies is to move from traditional IBTs to VDT structures, whereby the lower prices for smaller consumption levels can be obtained only by those households that consume very little and are more likely to be poor. Although this was not shown in this chapter, in most cases, this would have only a limited impact on targeting performance, but it would help in reducing the amount of subsidies allocated by governments to piped water consumption. Another alternative would be to provide connection as opposed to consumption subsidies, assuming that the production and distribution capacity is sufficient to expand the network.

The simulations implemented in this chapter suggest that this alternative could have a larger impact on targeting performance than simply changing at the margin the characteristics of tariffs.

References

Alleyne, T. 2013. *Energy Subsidy Reform in Sub-Saharan Africa: Experiences and Lessons.* Washington, DC: International Monetary Fund.

Angel-Urdinola, D., and Q. Wodon. 2007. "Do Utility Subsidies Reach the Poor? Framework and Evidence for Cape Verde, Sao Tome, and Rwanda." *Economics Bulletin* 9 (4): 1–7.

———. 2012. "Does Increasing Access to Infrastructure Services Improve the Targeting Performance of Water Subsidies?" *Journal of International Development* 24 (1): 88–101.

Banerjee, S., Q. Wodon, and V. Foster. 2010. "Dealing with Poverty and Inequality." In *Africa's Infrastructure: A Time for Transformation,* edited by V. Foster and C. Briceno-Garmendia. Washington, DC: Africa Development Forum, Agence Française de Développement and World Bank.

Estache, A., V. Foster, and Q. Wodon. 2002. *Accounting for Poverty in Infrastructure Reform: Learning from Latin America's Experience.* WBI Development Studies. Washington, DC: World Bank.

Estache, A., and Q. Wodon. 2014. *Infrastructure and Poverty in Sub-Saharan Africa.* New York: Palgrave Macmillan.

International Monetary Fund. 2013. *Case Studies on Energy Subsidy Reform: Lessons and Implications.* Washington, DC: International Monetary Fund.

Komives, K., V. Foster, J. Halpern, and Q. Wodon. 2005. *Water, Piped Water, and the Poor: Who Benefits from Utility Subsidies?* Directions in Development. Washington, DC: World Bank.

Lauria, D., and O. Hopkins. 2004. *Pro-Poor Subsidies for Water Connections: Cases from West Africa.* Chapel Hill: University of North Carolina.

Wodon, Q., M. I. Ajwad, and C. Siaens. 2003. "Lifeline or Means Testing? Electric Utility Subsidies in Honduras." In *Infrastructure for the Poor People: Public Policy for Private Provision,* edited by P. Brook and T. Irwin. Washington, DC: World Bank.

Ying, Y., H. Skilling, S. Banerjee, Q. Wodon, and V. Foster. 2010. "Cost Recovery, Equity, and Efficiency in Water Tariffs: Evidence from African Utilities." Policy Research Working Paper No. 5384, World Bank, Washington, D.C.

CHAPTER 7

Tariff Increase and Affordability

Clarence Tsimpo, Willy Kagarura, Nakafu Rose Kazibwe, John Ssenkumba Nsimbe, and Quentin Wodon

Introduction

In 2012, the price of piped water was increased by about 20 percent. This chapter assesses the impact of this increase in tariffs on households in terms of consumption, poverty, and affordability. The results suggest that the piped water tariff increase did not affect poverty in any substantial way, because so few households in poverty are connected. In addition, piped water appears to remain affordable for the households connected to the network. However, insights from qualitative fieldwork suggest that connection costs, as opposed to consumption costs, are an issue, with many households living in areas with network coverage not able to connect in part because of those costs.

Access to piped water provides a range of benefits for households and communities, as well as society as a whole. Piped water is safe, and thereby reduces morbidity in the population as a whole and especially among children, saving lives. The cost of piped water for households is often lower than the cost of relying on alternatives, at least in urban areas. In comparison to other water sources, access to piped water generates time savings for household members that can be reallocated to productive use. For these and many other reasons, and in order to promote affordability, many governments in developing countries provide subsidies for residential piped water. This is done either for consumption through tariff structures that may not fully reflect cost or for network expansion. Yet these subsidies are often badly targeted to the poor (e.g., Banerjee et al. 2010; Estache and Wodon 2014). In Uganda, these subsidies, to the extent they exist, are limited but at least in the case of consumption subsidies, it can be shown that they are poorly targeted to those in need (on the piped water sector in Uganda and recent reforms, see among others Mawejje et al. 2012 and Mwaura 2012).

To avoid subsidizing consumption and reflect costs of delivery, the government of Uganda increased tariffs for piped water in 2012. The first section of this chapter relies on the 2012/13 Uganda National Household survey to analyze the impact of this decision on households. The results suggest that the piped water tariff increase did not affect poverty in any substantial way, because so few households in poverty are connected. In addition, piped water appears to remain affordable for the households connected to the network.

However, this does not mean that affordability issues do not arise with access to safe water in general, and piped water in particular. Insights from qualitative fieldwork related to water and sanitation[1] suggest that connection costs, as opposed to consumption tariffs, may be an issue with many households living in areas with network coverage not able to connect in part because of those connection costs. The qualitative fieldwork on which this assessment is based was undertaken in 14 districts selected in such a way that at least one district was sampled from each geographical subregion of Uganda. In each region, districts were randomly selected from areas with varied water and sanitation performance grading in order to include good, fair, and poor performing areas in terms of access to safe water in the sample. In addition, purposive targeting was used to select and include districts reflecting some of the main livelihood clusters (pastoralists, crop farmers, fishing) for household. Finally, in each district two communities, one urban and one rural, were visited. While these districts are not representative of Uganda as a country, they tend to be illustrative of some of its poorer areas.

The chapter is organized as follows. Section 2 provides results from the microeconomic analysis of the impact of the 2012 tariff increase on household consumption, poverty, and affordability using the 2012/13 survey. Section 3 discusses results from qualitative fieldwork that relates to piped water with a focus on connection costs to the network. A conclusion follows.

Household Survey Analysis

Two types of microeconomic analysis of household survey data are performed. First, the impact of the increase in piped water tariffs on national welfare (consumption per equivalent adult) and poverty measures is estimated. Second, the impact of the tariff increases on the affordability of piped water for those households connected to the network is discussed.

Table 7.1 provides the tariffs that prevailed before the increase and the new tariff adopted as of 2012. At the time of the implementation of the 2009/10 Uganda National Household Survey, the unit cost per cubic meter was U Sh 1,585. This increased to U Sh 1,912 at the time of the 2012/13 survey, representing a 20.6 percent increase in unit price. As shown in figure 7.1, which provides the density functions of piped water consumption estimated with the two surveys, most households consume well below 15 cubic meters per month in both years (there does not seem to have been any large reduction in consumption by

Table 7.1 Residential Piped Water, 2009/10 and 2012/13

Year	Cost (U Sh)
2009/10	1,585
2012/13	1,912

Source: National Water and Sewerage Corporation (NWSC).
Note: The tariff was a flat rate per cubic meter. Service charge was not included (U Sh 1,500 in 2012/13).

Figure 7.1 Distribution of Piped Water Consumption, 2009/10 and 2012/13

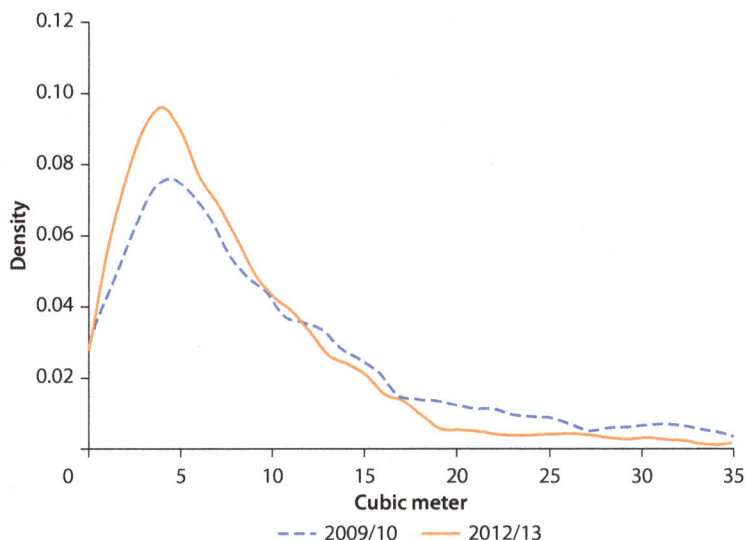

Source: Uganda 2012/13 UNHS.

households after the tariff increase). These relatively low levels of consumption mean that the absolute increase in cost due to the change in unit prices has been below U Sh 5,000 per month for most households.

To keep things simple, the assessment of the impact on poverty of the increase in tariffs is done in a simplified way. Denote by Y_i the consumption per equivalent adult of household i and by E_i^{t2} its spending on piped water in the second period $t2$ (the survey year 2012/13). Assume that there has been no change in piped water consumption due to the tariff increase. This is equivalent to assuming a zero price elasticity, thereby overstating the negative impact on households of the change in piped water tariffs. Then the level of welfare that the household could have experienced without the tariff increase is computed as E_i^{t1} with $E_i^{t1} < E_i^{t2}$.

Denoting N_i the household size (in terms of the number of equivalent adults in the household), and noting that without the tariff increase the household would have been able to spend $E_i^{t2} - E_i^{t1}$ on other goods, the counterfactual consumption per equivalent adult without tariff increase Y_i^C is computed as follows:

$$Y_i^C = Y_i + \frac{E_i^{t2} - E_i^{t1}}{N_i}$$

Standard FGT poverty measures (Foster, Greer et Thorbecke, 1984) are then used to estimate the impact of the change in tariffs among households connected to the network and among the population as a whole. Denoting the poverty line by Z, and the size of the population by n, the poverty measures with (P) and without (P^C) the change in tariffs are estimated as follows:

$$P = \frac{1}{n}\sum_{i=1}^{n}1_{Z>Y_i}\left[\frac{Z-Y_i}{Z}\right]^{\alpha} \quad \text{and} \quad P^C = \frac{1}{n}\sum_{i=1}^{n}1_{Z>Y_i}\left[\frac{Z-Y_i^C}{Z}\right]^{\alpha}$$

The headcount index of poverty is obtained for α equal to zero, the poverty gap for α equal to one, and the squared poverty gap for α equal to two. While the headcount index provides the share of the population in poverty, the poverty gap takes into account the distance separating the poor from the poverty lines, as well as the proportion of the poor in the population, and the squared poverty gap is based on the square of that distance. More sophisticated methods could be used to measure the general equilibrium effect of the increase in tariffs (including for commercial and industrial customers), and these are discussed in the next section, but the estimations given in this section provide a quick "first round" welfare (consumption) and poverty effects from higher tariffs paid directly by households for their piped water consumption. Again, because we have assumed no price elasticity, the effects tend to be overestimated.

The results of the simulations are provided in table 7.2. There is simply no impact on poverty because in the 2012/13 survey there are essentially no poor households connected to the network in the sample (and a few households in the sample that declare being connected also declare not paying for their consumption). Since there is no impact on poverty among connected households, there is also no impact for the population as a whole, as shown in table 7.2. In other words, the progressive reduction in poverty measures over time, including over the last few years, and the persistent low rate of piped water coverage have combined to reduce even more than before the number of poor households that are connected to the network.

The effects of the tariff increase on the consumption aggregate are a bit more visible in table 7.2, and these are provided for the sample of connected households, as well as nationally. But these effects on consumption are very mild with the simulated counterfactual consumption without the tariff increase only very slightly above consumption without the increase.

Why are those effects on welfare (consumption) and poverty so small? Because few households are connected, and among those virtually none in poverty, but also because, as shown in figure 7.2, the average piped water burden (the share of household consumption allocated to piped water) is small for those

Table 7.2 Impact of the Tariff Increase on Consumption and Poverty

| | Connected households | | | | National population | | | |
| | Consumption per equivalent adult | | Consumption per equivalent adult | | Poverty headcount | | Poverty gap | |
	Actual	Simulated	Actual	Simulated	Actual	Simulated	Actual	Simulated
Area								
Rural	147,035	147,109	56,008	56,009	22.35	22.35	5.92	5.92
Urban	166,211	166,422	109,400	109,444	9.63	9.63	2.54	2.54
Region								
Central	187,195	187,425	103,781	103,810	5.12	5.12	1.03	1.03
Eastern	122,209	122,377	51,036	51,042	24.08	24.08	5.26	5.26
Northern	123,953	124,181	42,902	42,905	43.76	43.76	14.18	14.18
Western	138,910	139,005	72,995	72,999	7.63	7.63	1.47	1.47
National	163,341	163,532	68,082	68,093	19.48	19.48	5.16	5.16

Source: Uganda 2012/13 UNHS.

Figure 7.2 Average Piped Water Burden among Connected Households, by Decile

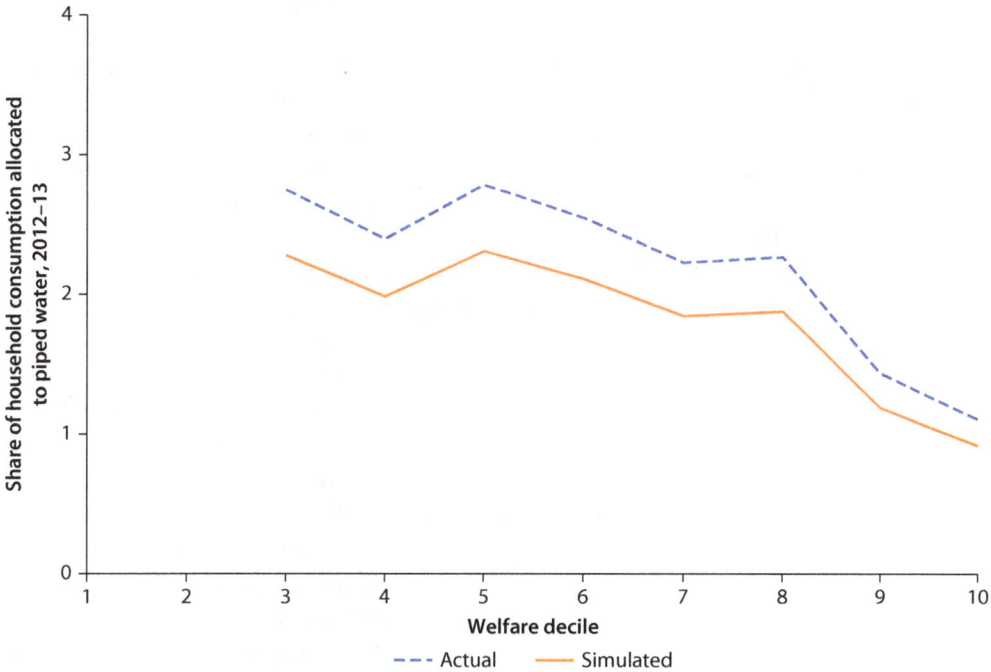

Source: Uganda 2012/13 UNHS.

connected, at between 1 and 3 percent in 2012/13 depending on the decile of consumption of the household (and even less under the counterfactual of no tariff increase). As a rule of thumb, the cost of network consumption is often considered as affordable if the burden it represents as a share of household budgets is below 5 percent. Figure 7.2 shows that this is clearly the case at least on average by decile of overall consumption in Uganda for those households who are connected to the network.

Does this mean that piped water is affordable for all households connected to the network and even perhaps for those not connected, assuming they might be able to connect at some point? Not necessarily. What is considered affordable is a normative judgment, but as just mentioned it is often suggested that the piped water bill of a household should ideally not exceed 5 percent of its total consumption. In figures 7.3 to 7.6, we provide estimates of the share of the various groups in the population for which the piped water bill would represent a burden considered "too high" (that is, more than 5 percent of their total consumption) under different scenarios as to the unit price of piped water (on the horizontal axis). To assess affordability, we consider that the minimum level of consumption that a household should be able to afford is five cubic meters per month, a fairly low "lifeline".

Consider figure 7.3 for the population as a whole, comparing the last two survey years for 2009/10 and 2012/13. The higher curve in the figure is for the year 2009/10, and the curve for 2012/13 is well below, suggesting substantial improvements in affordability between the two years, essentially because this was a period of economic growth in which consumption levels for households increased (and poverty was reduced). Given the unit price of U Sh 1,912 per cubic meter in 2012/13, the cost of a 5 cubic meter level of consumption per month would not be affordable (that is, would represent a burden of more than 5 percent of total household consumption) for less than a fifth of households in 2012/13 in the population as a whole.

However, when considering only households with a connection to the network, the curves are much lower since that population group tends to have much higher levels of consumption than the population as a whole. As shown in figure 7.4, at current unit prices, a consumption of 5 cubic meters per month would not be affordable for less than 5 percent of connected households in 2012/13. Figures 7.5 and 7.6 provide the same information for two other groups of households: those with access in their area but no connection and those without access in their area. The curves for those without access in their area are somewhat similar to those for the population. The curves for those with access in their area but no connection suggest that at current prices a consumption of 5 cubic meters per month would not be affordable for about 1 in 10 households in that group. Thus, there would be some households potentially facing an affordability issue, as defined here in terms of burden, if connections were made available to that group, but for a large majority of households, the service would be affordable, and willingness to pay studies suggest that many households would be willing to pay in order to have the service.

Figure 7.3 Affordability of Piped Water, Population as a Whole

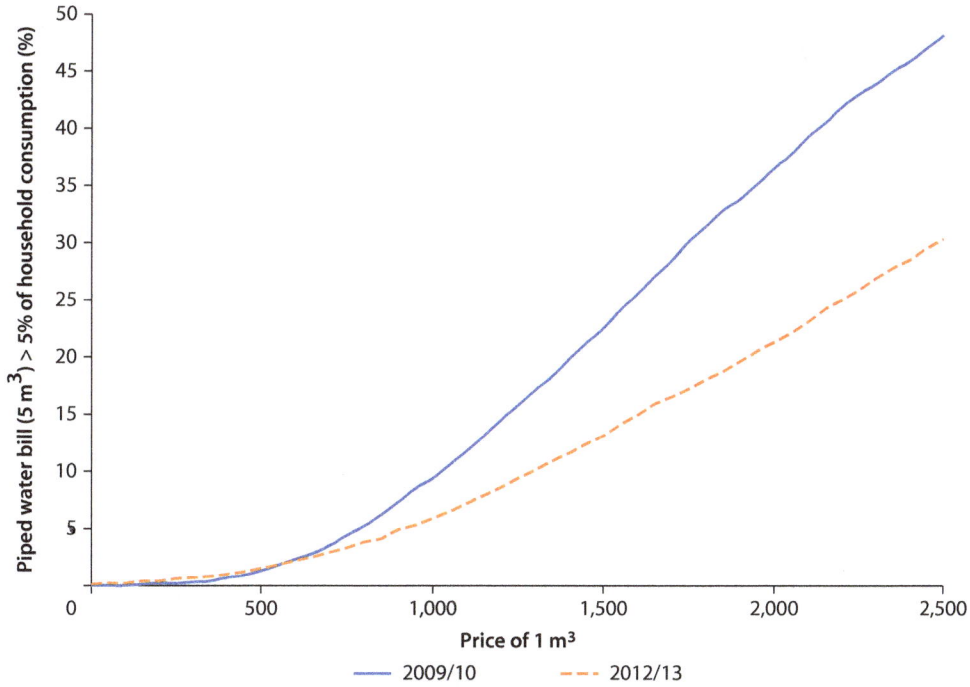

Source: Uganda 2009/10 and 2012/13 UNHS survey.

Figure 7.4 Affordability of Piped Water, Connected Households

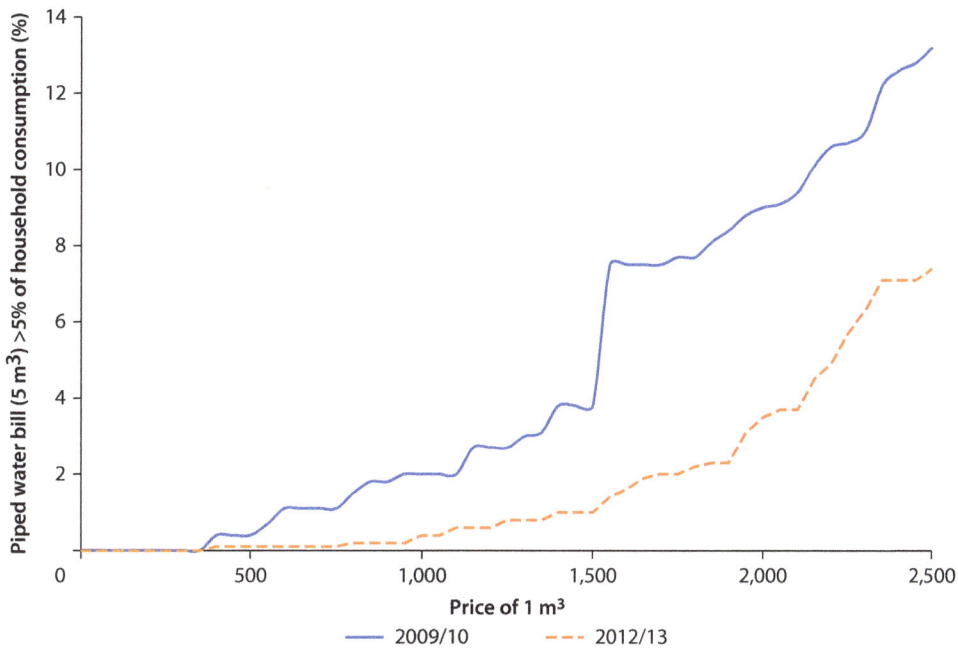

Source: Uganda 2009/10 and 2012/13 UNHS survey.

Residential Piped Water in Uganda • http://dx.doi.org/10.1596/978-1-4648-0708-4

Figure 7.5 Affordability of Piped Water, Households with Access and No Connection

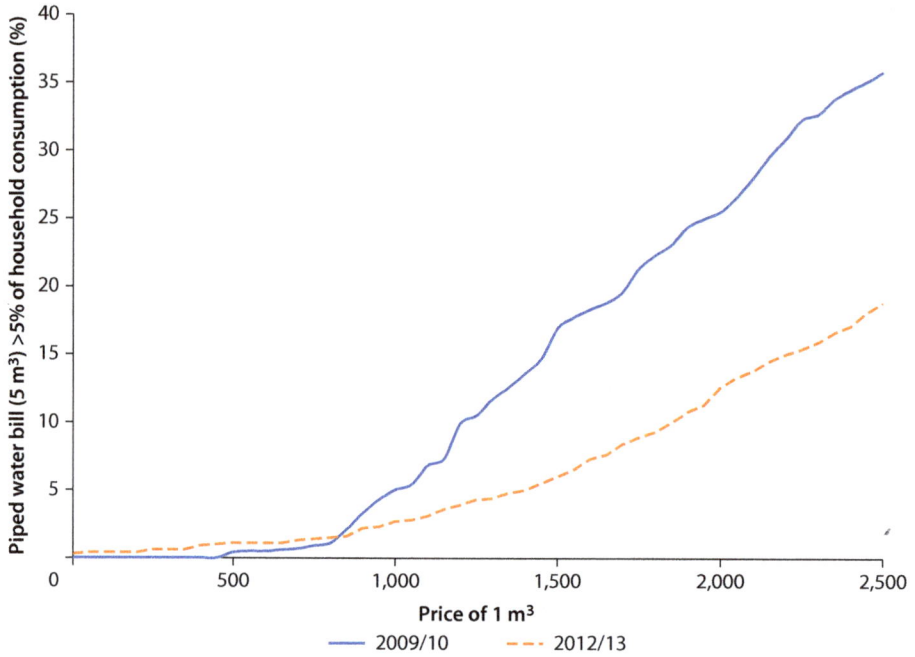

Source: Authors using Uganda 2009/10 and 2012/13 UNHS survey.

Figure 7.6 Affordability of Piped Water, Households without Access

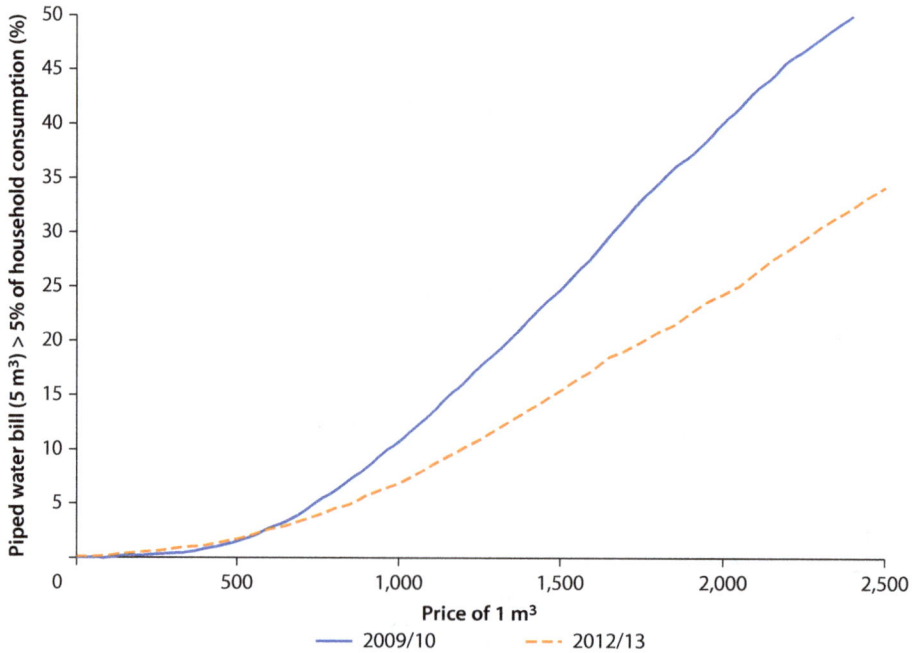

Source: Uganda 2009/10 and 2012/13 UNHS survey.

The upshot of the microeconomic analysis presented in this section is that (i) there was virtually no impact of the increase in piped water tariffs on poverty in Uganda; (ii) the impact on welfare as measured by consumption per equivalent adult is very mild; (iii) for only 1 in 20 households connected to the network, piped water seems not to be affordable according to commonly used burden metrics; and (iv) for about 9 in 10 households with access to network in their area but no connection, piped water should be affordable at current unit costs. This is not too surprising, and a similar conclusion has been reached by Sendegeya et al. (2009), who show that previous tariff increases were considered as acceptable by households.

Qualitative Fieldwork

The analysis in the previous section suggests that when considering all households with a connection to the water network, consumption tariffs seem affordable overall, and the 2012 increase in tariffs did not have any significant impact on poverty measures simply because most households in poverty are not connected to the network. This does not mean however that water is affordable for all, especially in terms of the cost of connecting to the network.

As mentioned in the introduction, qualitative fieldwork was conducted in 14 districts as part of a broader analysis of water and sanitation issues in Uganda, and some of the results from the qualitative data provide additional insights into the affordability of water for the population. Respondents in the fieldwork suggested that cost, as well as issues related to functionality, distance, quality, and seasonality remained factors preventing access to safe water for some households. They mentioned that during dry spells natural water sources dry up or have such a reduced flow that people must find alternative sources of water, which in most cases have a cost. Some buy water from vendors at a high price or go to public taps where the cost of water can be high despite subsidies provided by the National Water and Sewerage Corporation (NWSC).

Piped water was found in the urban areas of all 14 districts visited for the qualitative fieldwork. In some areas, as was the case for areas visited in Apac District, the presence of NWSC is recent (six months only). NWSC came to operate the network after a failure of the private operator. The operator had closed shop for two years, leading Apac District leaders to lobby for NWSC to overtake the network. The assessment by the NWSC manager of the ability to pay by community members was optimistically high, noting that NWSC had been able to collect 90 percent of the charges billed to households. Yet, some institutions, including the local health center, were in arrears in part because they allowed community members to fetch water from the taps essentially for free at the facility. Even though the allocation per household is small, this builds up. By contrast, government schools have been paying their water bill with ease according to the NWSC manager. The structure of payments for police, prisons, and army is different, following a centralized payment of bills through an office in Kampala.

When asked about the quality of the services provided by NWSC, respondents were quick to say that the corporation is very responsive to customer complaints and ensures quick and immediate redress. The corporation also has a culture of adhering to strict targets, which helps for continued employment for its workers, but those who may not meet collection targets may be fired. The performance of water kiosks was also said to have improved a bit after since NWSC took over the water network. Finally, the fees paid for water are reasonable.

Issues were however raised about the ability of NWSC to supply enough water, and the cost of connecting to the network. In the municipality of Gulu where piped water needs were estimated at 5,000 cubic meters, NWSC was said to be able to supply only 3,500 cubic meters at most. Other challenges for the supply of water include intermittent power interruptions, breakdown of generators needed for pumping the water, and damage to pipes due to road works. But the main complaint has been with high connection fees that limit access to water considered safe. Respondents felt that water connection should be made easier for community members so that a larger number of households could access water at a minimal and affordable price.

The cost of connecting to the network seems to vary from place to place, which may be related to the fact that different operators are covering different areas in small towns. In some towns, the initial fee for a connection is U Sh 50,000 shillings. In addition, households requesting a 0.5 inch pipe connection are charged U Sh 105,000 shillings and those requesting a 0.75 inch pipe are charged U Sh210,000. But while the cost of pipes for those located close from the main tends to be included in the fees, extra distance has to be paid for, which may make connection costs unaffordable for many. A man in Kisoro explained that *"one has to have about U Sh 780,000 to complete the whole process of water connection on top of paying U Sh 50,000 as connection fee, and then one must later pay the water charges. This is a lot of money and more than half of the population in the whole town council can't afford it."* He added that *"NWSC is no longer focusing on helping the community to access safe water but it has turned into a profit making organization."* Another man in Moyo stated it: *"Registration to be connected requires 50,000 Shillings that is supposed to be deposited at the sub-county. Connection pipes of 200 meters cost an additional 350,000 Shillings. This is not affordable by most of the residents."*

The issue of households being disconnected, even for small unpaid bills, was also raised by respondents. As an elderly woman in Kisoro District explained it: *"We thought that the problem of water will be solved with the coming of NWSC but this has not been the case since their main focus is disconnecting people even if the unpaid bill is as low as U Sh 500, yet for one to get reconnected, you have to pay a charge of U Sh 11,000, which is as well too much."* Finally, some households feel that they may be charged too much by utilities—whether NWSC or local operators, and many do not know how to read their bill and meter. High levels of charges in some areas were mentioned, irrespective of potentially long periods when taps may be dry.

Another issue that was mentioned, but not about NWSC, is that some private contractors prefer not to be supervised by Water Department staff when they are constructing new water sources, which usually results in poor standards of work. They tend to ignore ministry technical staffs and go directly to politicians. But at the end they try to seek certification of the quality of work from the Water Department, and it may not be granted then. The issue is that politicians tend not to follow technical criteria to select the location of water sources. In some areas, there are also conflicts about where to locate water points, which may cause delays.

Conclusion

This chapter suggests that the impact of the 2012 network tariff increase on households has been small. The results suggest that the piped water tariff increase did not affect poverty in any substantial way, because so few households in poverty are connected. In addition, piped water appears to remain affordable for the households connected to the network, and it would also be affordable for most households living in areas with access (as measured in the surveys) but not yet connected. However, insights from qualitative fieldwork suggest that connection costs, as opposed to consumption costs, are an issue, with many households living in areas with network coverage not able to connect in part because of those costs.

Finally, although this has not been discussed here, it can be shown that the cost of water obtained by households from public stand pipes may be higher than it should, and access to safe water remains an issue for many households not connected to the network.

Note

1. The instruments used for the fieldwork included focus-group discussions (FGDs), key informant interviews, observations, and case studies. Before fieldwork activities, detailed checklists for FGDs and case studies were developed to guide the different categories of targeted populations. The categories of stakeholders that were targeted for data collection included community members (women, men, youth, elderly), leaders of water user committees, local government officials (CAOs, district water officers, district health inspectors, district health educators), and at the national level officials of National Water and Sewerage Corporation, Ministry of Water and Environment, Ministry of Health officials, and Kampala Divisions Health Inspectors. Some visits to health centres and schools were also conducted to provide a physical assessment of the toilet facilities and provisions for hand washing, with observations and photographs made on site. Visits were also done to water projects such as dams and pumping sites.

References

Banerjee, S., Q. Wodon, and V. Foster. 2010. "Dealing with Poverty and Inequality." In *Africa's Infrastructure: A Time for Transformation*, edited by V. Foster and C. Briceno-Garmendia. Washington, DC: Africa Development Forum, Agence Française de Développement and World Bank.

Estache, A., and Q. Wodon. 2014. *Infrastructure and Poverty in Sub-Saharan Africa.* New York: Palgrave Macmillan.

Foster, J. E., J. Greer, and E. Thorbecke. 1984. "A Class of Decomposable Poverty Indices." *Econometrica* 52: 761–66.

Mawejje, J., E. Munyambonera, and L. Bategeka. 2012. "Uganda's Piped Water Reforms and Institutional Restructuring." Economic Policy Research Centre Working Paper No. 89, Kampala, Uganda.

Mwaura, F. M. 2012. "Adopting Piped Water Prepayment Billing System to Reduce Non-technical Losses in Uganda: Lessons from Rwanda." *Utilities Policy 23*, 72–79.

Sendegeya, A., E. Lugujjo, I. P. Da Silva, L. Soder, and M. Amelin. 2009. "Application of Price Sensitivity Measurement Method to Assess the Acceptance of Piped Water Tariffs: A Case Study in Uganda." IEEE AFRICON 2009, 23–25 September 2009, Nairobi, Kenya.